Purposeful Grieving

Embracing God's Plan in the Midst of Loss

Stacy E. Hoehl, Ph.D.

NORTHWESTERN PUBLISHING HOUSE
Milwaukee, Wisconsin

Cover Photo: iStockphoto LP
Interior Photos: Lightstock
Art Director: Lynda Williams
Design Team: Diane Cook, Pamela Dunn

Northwestern Publishing House
N16W23379 Stone Ridge Dr., Waukesha, WI 53188-1108
www.nph.net
© 2019 Northwestern Publishing House
Published 2019
Printed in the United States of America
ISBN 978-0-8100-3006-0
ISBN 978-0-8100-3007-7 (e-book)

23 24 25 26 27 28   10 9 8 7 6 5 4 3

Contents

Dear Grieving Heart,

"I'm sorry for your loss." Have you heard those words a lot lately? I'm sure you've heard that sentiment expressed regularly—especially if your grief is fresh. For most non-grievers, this short sentence serves as a polite way of consoling someone when better words are hard to find. It communicates regret about what the grieving person is going through.

But we can't change what has happened. We can't reverse the loss. Regret and sorrow look to the past and expend their energy in the wrong direction. Now, I understand that it would sound too harsh if I said that I'm not sorry for your loss. Instead, I will share this encouragement from my personal grieving experiences: God can use our seasons of loss to bring about gains we may never have imagined, and I'm not sorry that God has the opportunity to showcase his power and wisdom in your life. I also believe it's possible to work through these times of grief in a slow, take-all-the-time-you-need fashion that faces forward with full trust in God's promises. This is Purposeful Grieving.

Each day, these devotions will offer you a brief message about the experience of grief, along with relevant words of comfort from the Bible. Take your time reading the devotions; encourage yourself to answer questions along the way, and truly connect my experiences to your own. At the end of each message, you'll find a prayer and two journaling sections called Reflect and Release. You can use these prompts as a journal of your path of healing or as conversation starters for you and your spouse or a trusted friend. The Reflect questions will challenge you to wrestle further with the day's message and what it means for you in your grieving process. Finally, the Release section contains a thought to ponder, a prayer strategy to use, or an action to complete as God

works in your heart while you're grieving. I have found it
personally helpful to have something to do *with my grief.*
Again, this is Purposeful Grieving. *Actively reframing*
your thoughts, identifying your emotions, and reaching
out to others are intentional strategies that will help you
embrace God's will for your life—even in the midst of loss.

My prayers are with you as you engage in Purposeful Grieving!

Yours truly,
Stacy

WEEK 1

DAY 1 Starting Together

As we embark together on this journey through the grieving process, I begin with a heartfelt appeal to your sense of commitment. Are you with me? Working through grief is a long, challenging process, but it is worth doing well. My prayer is that God will use these devotions to hold you, comfort you, strengthen you, and heal you as you simultaneously mourn the loss of your loved one and rejoice in God's promise of heaven for those who believe. Stay with me.

I've structured our devotions according to the pattern of a powerful psalm, Psalm 13. In my own experiences with grief, this psalm beautifully captured the stages I went through as I dealt with my own emotions while in the arms of my loving God. Focusing on a short portion of Psalm 13 as the theme for each week, the devotions will encourage us to acknowledge the emotions that surge within us and to find comfort in the tender heart of God.

Today I invite you to read the entire psalm slowly, taking the time to pause for reflection after each verse.

> *¹ How long, Lord? Will you forget me forever?*
> *How long will you hide your face from me?*

> ^{2} *How long must I wrestle with my thoughts*
> *and day after day have sorrow in my heart?*
> *How long will my enemy triumph over me?*
>
> ^{3} *Look on me and answer, LORD my God.*
> *Give light to my eyes, or I will sleep in death,*
>
> ^{4} *and my enemy will say, "I have overcome him,"*
> *and my foes will rejoice when I fall.*
>
> ^{5} *But I trust in your unfailing love;*
> *my heart rejoices in your salvation.*
>
> ^{6} *I will sing the LORD's praise,*
> *for he has been good to me. (Psalm 13)*

If you look closely at this psalm, you will notice that a transformation takes place. At the beginning, the author is wrestling with God and is very nearly in a state of despair. By the end, you can hear the optimism in his voice and the anticipation that he will be singing praises to the Lord for all the good things the Lord had done for him.

The rest of the devotions for this first week will focus on verse 1 of the psalm. We'll go back to those early moments of grief—when we too were very near despair, filled with shock and anger, and plagued by questions for God. We'll work through those feelings again, but with our eyes fixed on the empty cross of our risen Savior. His commitment to us inspires our commitment to him. Together we will grow spiritually, physically, and emotionally, that we might be better instruments to serve our Lord! Are you with me?

Prayer: *Dear heavenly Father, prepare my heart for this grieving process. Give me the strength and courage to grieve fully during this time of loss, knowing that you are refining me every step of the way. My worries, fears, and sadness can pull my focus away from you; help me to trust you completely! Amen.*

▨ **Reflect:** What overwhelms you the most about your grief? Can you identify any fears or worries that keep you from letting yourself fully grieve your loss? Share these concerns with your loving Father in heaven.

▨ **Release:** Set aside a dedicated time each day to work through these devotions as part of your grieving process. How can you build a ritual into your day that will keep you committed to the process? For example, do you have a quiet room that you can retreat to during your devotion time? Can you enhance that space (with music, a fragrant candle, a cup of tea, etc.) so that it relaxes and comforts you?

DAY 2 | How Long, Lord?

Were you one of those kids who called out from the back seat of the car, "Are we there yet?" Or do you hear that question from your children? I know I've asked, "Are we there yet?" out of impatience, frustration, and anxiousness. And I can vividly recall the physical feeling of being trapped in the car, my legs screaming for the chance to stretch and run around.

Our theme this week focuses on the earliest stage of grief—the shock, denial, anger, and questioning that occur as our immediate response to the loss. We'll cry along with the psalmist, "How long, LORD? Will you forget me forever? How long will you hide your face from me?" (Psalm 13:1). When David wrote these words, he was expressing the intensity of his emotions—his anguish.

When we first face loss and experience grief, similar emotions saturate our thoughts and compel us to ask the same kinds of questions: How long will I feel like this? How long will I feel forsaken by God? Why does God feel so far away? During the earliest moments of grief, it is the most difficult to see God's hand at work and to understand his purpose. When the tears are still in our eyes, it's difficult to see beyond the wet, blurry mess. And when we can't see out, we feel forsaken—as if no one is looking in.

Even Christ experienced the feeling of being forsaken by God. On the cross, our Savior cried, "My God, my God, why have you forsaken me?" But even as Christ asked the question, God's hand was at work and his purpose was being accomplished. Christ was forsaken so that our sins would be forgiven. Christ was rejected so that we would be redeemed.

In our moments of impatience when we anxiously ask God, "Are we there yet?" let us remember that God's hand is at work and his purpose is being accomplished in us. Thy will be done.

Prayer: *Dear heavenly Father, thank you for accomplishing your great purpose in my life. Fill me with a trusting spirit when I am tempted to doubt. Lead me, Lord; I will follow you. Amen.*

■ **Reflect:** What are your impatient questions right now? What are you most frustrated about during these early stages of grief?

■ **Release:** What do you most want God to know about your feelings right now? Keep a running list of these thoughts or feelings as they occur to you. During your moments of prayer, return to the list and lay your concerns before your loving God.

DAY 3 Numb

When I was preparing for labor and the delivery of our first child, my husband and I bought a video that was supposed to guide us through some relaxation techniques and coping strategies. It started out with some good suggestions, but then things got strange. The labor and delivery coach asked us to get a few ice cubes from the freezer. She told us to hold the ice cubes in our hands for three minutes and then to use our newfound relaxation techniques to cope with the pain. Though the exercise felt silly at first, it didn't take long before a sharp, needling pain set in.

I'm still drawing lessons from that icy experience today, and I'd like to share some with you. I remember that numb feeling in my hands incredibly well. It was a shock to my hands. It was hard to think about anything else. It left me longing for the moment relief would come. As I deal with the grief surrounding my recurrent pregnancy loss and the loss of several close relatives, I often experience the same sensations. Perhaps you do too. We won't forget our experiences with grief; we remember them well. Loss is a shock to our systems. It's hard for us to think about anything else. And loss leaves us longing for a moment of relief—the reaction expressed by the psalm writer in our verse for this week: "How long, LORD? Will you forget me forever? How long will you hide your face from me?" (Psalm 13:1).

What is the purpose of the numbness that blankets us after we experience loss? What good can come from those feelings? What does God accomplish in us through them? The numbness may be God's blessing to spare us from the pain that would otherwise be too sharp for us to bear. In the meantime, God is working in our hearts. Second Corinthians 4:16-18 helps us understand what God is accomplishing. As you read these verses, pay careful attention to the comparison in verse 16 between bodily, physical feelings and God's care for our souls: "Therefore we do not lose heart.

Though outwardly we are wasting away, yet inwardly we are being renewed day by day." Though we feel numb with grief—like we are wasting away—God has the power to renew us every day with the warmth of his love.

Next, when grief shocks our systems, God offers us his consistency and security. Verses 17,18 read: "For our light and momentary troubles are achieving for us an eternal glory that far outweighs them all. So we fix our eyes not on what is seen, but on what is unseen, since what is seen is temporary, but what is unseen is eternal." Over and above all of our earthly experiences, God has our eternal good in mind. Though we feel shaken, God is a steady, eternal refuge! When our life seems to be crumbling beneath us, we fix our eyes on his eternal promises.

Finally, we realize that we experience grief as a result of sin. But God gives us the promise of eternal life through Jesus Christ. Jesus completely washed away the power of sin and death, and the numbness and grief, with his blood. Indeed, the eternal glory that we will experience with God outweighs what we're going through on this earth!

So, to prepare yourself for handling your grief or for facing any difficult situation, don't go looking in the freezer. God wants to draw you near and to renew you through his grace. God is there. He always will be. And he will be waiting for you in eternal glory. Let's fix our eyes heavenward!

Prayer: *Heavenly Father, accomplish your will in me. Use this time of grief to draw me closer to you. Thank you for the promise of your Son and the hope of heaven. Amen.*

▨ **Reflect:** How have you experienced the numbness of grief thus far? Emotionally? Physically? Spiritually?

Can you identify the unproductive ways that you've tried to "fix" the numbness in your life?

■ **Release:** What's one thought from today's devotion that can help you refocus your eyes on God's *eternal* plan for you?

DAY 4 Kicking and Screaming

Where was the worst tantrum you've ever witnessed? the grocery store checkout line? your own living room? on a playground somewhere? No matter the location, we've all seen some pretty dramatic tantrums. Arms flailing, legs kicking, fists pounding, feet stomping. Vocal sounds we never thought possible. As I've witnessed tantrums, I've found myself silently chiding the little one and thinking, *Give it up.*

Yes, most of the time, we assume that a tantrum performance is given by a child. But, if I'm honest with myself, I have to admit that I've been guilty of the kicking and screaming behaviors that accompany the worst of tantrums. Perhaps my tantrums haven't been public outbursts or physical demonstrations, but that's not the point. People erupt when they feel that their freedoms have been violated, that they can't have something they deserve, or that something isn't fair. Yep, I've been there during this grieving process. Have you?

As I picture myself kicking and screaming against the will of God, I can also picture my Father in heaven looking at me and thinking, *Give it up.* Literally! God wants us to give up fighting against his will. When we kick and scream, we're really questioning whether God knows what is right or, when you get right down to it, we are telling him that he doesn't. He wants us to trust him. He wants us to rest in the knowledge that his hands hold our lives firmly in their grasp. Read what God tells us in Isaiah 41:10,13: "Do not fear, for I am with you; do not be dismayed, for I am your God. I will strengthen you and help you; I will uphold you with my righteous right hand. For I am the LORD your God who takes hold of your right hand and says to you, Do not fear; I will help you."

Our heavenly Father waits for us with his arms wide open. He patiently and persistently invites us to come to him for the help and strength we need.

So how shall we respond to our Lord's invitation? First, let's repent of the sinful thoughts, words, and actions we've expressed with our tantrums. Let's let go of our need to ask, "How long, LORD?" and surrender to God's timing. Remember Jesus' words in Matthew 11:28: "Come to me, all you who are weary and burdened, and I will give you rest." Jesus is right there with the promise of forgiveness and rest for our souls. He's there with the promise of his empty cross. And he's there with the promise of eternity. Wow, I am in awe of his goodness.

Remember the reasons for our tantrums? They sure don't apply when we look forward to the hope of heaven.

Through Christ, I have more freedom than ever. Through Christ, I get more than I deserve. It isn't fair that Christ had to take my punishment, but because he did, he has declared my victory over death! Through Christ, I can let go of the earthly pains that haunt me and truly *give it up!*

Prayer: *Dear heavenly Father, forgive me for my tantrums. Forgive me for resisting your will and thinking that I know better. Lead me to trust in your will and rest in your promises. Amen.*

▨ **Reflect:** Have you experienced any tantrums, internal or external, while grieving? How have you expressed these tantrums? Physically? Verbally? Internally?

■ **Release:** Take your tantrum to the Lord in prayer. How can you help yourself remember to run to God when you are feeling weary and burdened?

DAY 5 Hide-and-Seek

Perhaps remember playing hide-and-seek when you were a child and becoming exasperated when it felt like you would never find the person. I can remember. At that point, the role of "seeker" suddenly became a quite frustrating and lonely part to play. The game wasn't very fun. My eyes grew weary of the fruitless search. My imagination started running away from me. . . . *What if he/she just decided to quit the game and go inside?*

In Psalm 13:1, the verse that is the theme for this week, you can sense the exasperation in the psalmist's voice: "How long will you hide your face from me?"

During those moments when we ask God how long he will hide his face, we are expressing our exasperation, frustration, and loneliness. It's amazing how waiting for guidance, answers, and comfort can leave a person feeling so small. After reading through the psalms during my time of grief, my eyes have been opened to see how often they speak about hiding and seeking. The psalmists prayed that God would hide his face from their sins (Psalm 51:9), hide them from evil and wickedness (Psalm 64:2), or hide them in the shelter of his protection (Psalm 17:8; 27:5; 31:20). These verses all reflect on the certain truth that we can hide in the Lord and trust in his forgiveness and protection. But the psalmists also often lament that sometimes it feels like God is hiding his face. Or they fear that, because of their sins, he might hide his face from them.

- *Why, LORD, do you stand far off? Why do you hide yourself in times of trouble? (Psalm 10:1)*

- *Do not hide your face from me, do not turn your servant away in anger; you have been my helper. Do not reject me or forsake me, God my Savior. (Psalm 27:9)*

- *Why do you hide your face and forget our misery and oppression? (Psalm 44:24)*

- *Do not hide your face from your servant; answer me quickly, for I am in trouble. (Psalm 69:17)*

- *Why, LORD, do you reject me and hide your face from me? (Psalm 88:14)*

- *Do not hide your face from me when I am in distress. Turn your ear to me; when I call, answer me quickly. (Psalm 102:2)*

- *Answer me quickly, LORD; my spirit fails. Do not hide your face from me or I will be like those who go down to the pit. (Psalm 143:7)*

Isn't that remarkable? Look at all of the emotions that the psalmists experienced when they felt God was hiding from them! In our times of trouble, distress, misery, and failing spirits, we can feel as though God is hiding so far away. Like children playing hide-and-seek, we might get frustrated and impatient with the process. The game isn't over yet! Seek him boldly! Take your inspiration from the psalmists once again:

- *Those who know your name trust in you, for you, LORD, have never forsaken those who seek you. (Psalm 9:10)*

- *They will receive blessing from the LORD and vindication from God their Savior. Such is the generation of those who seek him, who seek your face, God of Jacob. (Psalm 24:5,6)*

- *My heart says of you, "Seek his face!" Your face, LORD, I will seek. (Psalm 27:8)*

- *The lions may grow weak and hungry, but those who seek the LORD lack no good thing. (Psalm 34:10)*

- *May all who seek you rejoice and be glad in you; may those who long for your saving help always say, "The LORD is great!" (Psalm 40:16)*

- *You, God, are my God, earnestly I seek you; I thirst for you, my whole being longs for you, in a dry and parched land where there is no water. (Psalm 63:1)*

- *Look to the LORD and his strength; seek his face always. (Psalm 105:4)*

God uses our life events to draw us into his Word and to draw us closer to himself. "Come near to God and he will come near to you" (James 4:8). It may seem like a long wait, but God uses the waiting time to teach us patience and perseverance. We cannot know the mind of God, but we do know that he shapes each and every one of us for his greater purpose. In his timing, he orchestrated the world's history. In his timing, he sent his only Son as the Savior of all people. In his timing, he will answer your questions. In his timing, you will see his face in heaven!

> **Prayer:** *Just a closer walk with thee,*
> *grant it, Jesus, is my plea,*
> *daily walking close to thee,*
> *let it be, dear Lord, let it be.*
>
> *I am weak, but thou art strong;*
> *Jesus, keep me from all wrong;*
> *I'll be satisfied as long*
> *as I walk, let me walk close to thee.*
>
> *Through this world of toil and snares,*
> *if I falter, Lord, who cares?*
> *Who with me my burden shares?*
> *None but Thee, dear Lord, none but Thee.*
>
> *When my feeble life is o'er,*
> *time for me will be no more;*
> *guide me gently, safely o'er*
> *to thy kingdom shore, to thy shore. Amen.*

Reflect: Have you felt that God is distant from you during this time? How would you describe those feelings?

Release: How can you make extra time in your day to seek the Lord, knowing that he will come closer to you in return?

DAY 6 | The Isolation of Pain

Suffering is a lonely place. In our grief, it's hard to believe that anyone can really understand exactly what we're going through. It's hard to believe that anyone else has had a similar experience. It's hard to believe that anyone wants to hear about our feelings, our reactions, our hopes, and our fears. When such thoughts run through a grieving person's mind, it's tempting to think we're better off trying to handle the grief alone; thus, the isolation of pain.

I remember these thoughts and feelings well. I remember thinking, *No one truly understands what I'm going through. Who wants to be bothered by my sadness and grief?* Though we may feel alone in our suffering, look at what Scripture says in Hebrews 4:14-16:

> *Therefore, since we have a great high priest who has ascended into heaven, Jesus the Son of God, let us hold firmly to the faith we profess. For we do not have a high priest who is unable to empathize with our weaknesses, but we have one who has been tempted in every way, just as we are—yet he did not sin. Let us then approach God's throne of grace with confidence, so that we may receive mercy and find grace to help us in our time of need.*

God certainly gave us family and friends to comfort us during times of trouble and to help carry our burdens. But sinful people produce imperfect results and may sometimes fall short of our needs and expectations. That's why the message in Hebrews chapter 4 is so important for us to remember. Christ has been to our point of suffering and beyond. Christ felt the loneliness and rejection of being separated from the Father for our sins. Christ conquered pain, suffering, and death so that we might have the hope of heaven! So rather than accepting interpersonal distance and silence as inevitable, approach the throne of grace with confidence! You will meet the perfect listener, the only one who can truly empathize and the one who will bestow on you the mercy and grace you long for during your time of need!

Prayer: *Dear Jesus, forgive me for becoming frustrated with the people around me who don't always understand my experiences. Thank you for the pain, suffering, and death that you endured for me. In you, I have someone who understands my pain perfectly. And in you, I have the promise of heaven! Amen.*

Reflect: In what ways have you been comforted by family and friends during your grief? In what ways have you been disappointed with their attempts to comfort you?

Release: Share what you're feeling today with God in prayer, knowing that he is a perfect listener. He is the only one who can provide exactly what you need during this time of grief.

DAY 7 Week 1: Concluding Thoughts

Congratulations on surviving your first week! I'm praying that the Lord used Psalm 13:1 to draw you closer to himself: "How long, LORD? Will you forget me forever? How long will you hide your face from me?" We've had some frank discussions about what it's like at the beginning of the grief cycle: the numbness and shock, the isolation, the questioning, the kicking and screaming, and our perceived distance from God.

But, through it all, we have come to a place of hope! Our numbness is warmed and our shock is calmed by our loving Savior. Our isolation is overcome by a God who connects with us at every point of our suffering. Our questions will be answered in his good time. Our kicking and screaming are settled by a merciful, gracious, and understanding Father. And through the whole process, God draws us ever closer to himself.

As you go about your day, meditate on the words of Psalm 119:49,50. They are an incredibly fitting conclusion to our first week together: "Remember your word to your servant, for you have given me hope. My comfort in my suffering is this: Your promise preserves my life."

During shaky, uncertain times, these verses remind us of the hope and comfort we find in God's Word. His promise of salvation through his Son, Jesus Christ, preserves our lives and renews our strength as we battle through grief one day at a time. Rest on God's promises, and rest in his arms.

Prayer: *Dear heavenly Father, thank you for leading me through this first week. Fill me with a spirit of power and perseverance as I continue down this path. I praise you for the hope you've given me through your Son, Jesus Christ! Amen.*

▨ **Reflect:** What did you feel was your lowest point of grief during this week? Your highest? Take a moment to identify what helped you out of the lowest moments and into a better frame of mind.

▨ **Release:** Write down a Bible verse or one of God's promises that brings you comfort. Recite this verse throughout your day as a reminder of the faithfulness of our God.

WEEK 2

DAY 1 How Long Must I Wrestle?

As we look at the theme verse for this week's devotions, it's clear that our wrestling isn't over yet. "How long must I wrestle with my thoughts and day after day have sorrow in my heart? How long will my enemy triumph over me?" (Psalm 13:2).

As our theme verse suggests, grief is a wrestling match. It's almost as if our emotions and needs wrestle against each other. Our need to acknowledge sadness contends with an almost overwhelming desire for joy. We fight to free ourselves from smothering negativity, while frantically seeking positivity. We take a very earthly human view of things while rejoicing in the hope of heaven. I remember those mental and emotional battles well, and I experience them still. Are you worn out from this wrestling match yet? The grieving person often wonders, *How long am I going to feel this way? How many days will go by before I can make it through the day without tears? When will I feel like myself again?*

To be honest, you won't feel like "yourself" again. But that's the point. God allows pain, suffering, and trials to touch our lives in order to change us, shape us, and equip us to be instruments of his kingdom. Meditate on the following prayer for a few moments:

> *May the God of peace, who through the blood*
> *of the eternal covenant brought back from the*

> *dead our Lord Jesus, that great Shepherd of the*
> *sheep, equip you with everything good for doing*
> *his will, and may he work in us what is pleasing*
> *to him, through Jesus Christ, to whom be glory*
> *for ever and ever. Amen. (Hebrews 13:20,21)*

God is equipping you with everything you need to fulfill his purpose for your life! Yes, weighed down by sadness, it's a struggle to fight the tears. But praise the Lord: He loves you *so much* that he puts his hands right on your heart and molds you to his exact specifications! Check out Zechariah 13:9: "I will refine them like silver and test them like gold. They will call on my name and I will answer them; I will say, 'They are my people,' and they will say, 'The LORD is our God.'"

Rest in the hands of the Lord. He will accomplish his good purpose in your life. It's okay to wrestle during your time of grief. But as you do, be confident that victory is yours through Jesus.

Prayer: *Dear Lord, forgive me for my impatience with the grieving process. Calm my heart and help me realize that my times are in your hands. In the name of Jesus, my Savior. Amen.*

▨ **Reflect:** What thoughts or feelings are at either end of your personal wrestling match of grief? How has your impatience with yourself during this process—and wondering when you will feel "normal" again—affected your relationships?

■ **Release:** Think about how God's hands are actively shaping you today. What might he be preparing you for? For example, is there someone you might reach out to today who is also experiencing grief?

DAY 2 The Child in Your Heart

Why is a mother's sorrow so enduring? This is my story and my greatest source of grief. But no matter the source of your loss, we can all relate to the space in our hearts that was filled by the loved one we lost. And we all ask, "How long will I have sorrow in my heart?"

A woman never forgets the moment she finds out she's pregnant. She starts to think differently, feel differently, and experience the world differently. Suddenly, her eyes are opened to a new dimension in her future, a future full of hope and possibilities. Perhaps she folds her hands toward her stomach, respecting the miracle that occurs inside. Perhaps she envisions the growing process and imagines the first heartbeat. The switch has been flipped. That child has entered her heart.

A mother never forgets her child. All of her senses are caught up in that relationship. Her touch builds trust. Her eyes communicate love, approval, and concern. Her ears listen. She knows the child's scent. Memories are made, smiles are exchanged, laughs are shared, and tears are shed during their relationship—no matter the duration. She forms hopes on behalf of the child. The child is in her heart.

To experience the loss of a pregnancy or a child is to experience heartbreak in the fullest sense of the word. The hopes are stopped short of reality. The senses are prematurely stripped of their responsibilities. The mother clings to the memories and searches them almost constantly.

Thus is the human response to sorrow and loss. In these lowest moments of our grief, hope might seem out of reach. In your quest for comfort, remember the words of Psalm 116:1-6:

> *I love the LORD, for he heard my voice; he heard*
> *my cry for mercy. Because he turned his ear to*
> *me, I will call on him as long as I live. The cords*

*of death entangled me, the anguish of the grave
came over me; I was overcome by distress and
sorrow. Then I called on the name of the LORD:
"LORD, save me!" The LORD is gracious and
righteous; our God is full of compassion. The
LORD protects the unwary; when I was brought
low, he saved me.*

When you cry out in sadness, the Lord hears your voice. When you feel entangled and overcome by your sorrow, the Lord looks at you with compassion. Your loving Savior has every one of your tears in his hands. He holds your broken heart. The loved one in your heart is now in his care. Most important, he met your greatest need as a sinful human being—he died so that you might live with him in eternity!

Prayer: *Dear heavenly Father, you know how my heart hurts. Comfort me in my sorrow, and lift my eyes to you. Shower me with your graciousness and compassion. Amen.*

Reflect: Read Psalm 116:1-6 again. How can you connect these verses to your grieving process so far? Can you relate to the psalmist's emotions?

Release: Close your eyes and remember the loved one you lost; try to include as many of your senses as you can. As you remember the smiles, laughs, tears, scents, and hugs, capture them with a spirit of joy and thankfulness. Hold that joy and gratitude in your heart today.

DAY 3 Empty Hands

Take a look at your hands. If you are a parent or caregiver, think of all of the activities that our hands help us perform. We wipe away tears. We brush hair. We apply bandages when necessary. We hug, squeeze, and comfort. We tickle. We clap them to cheer, and pat on the back to congratulate. In all of these moments, our hands are an extension of our desire to nurture and care for our loved ones.

One of the most difficult and painful thoughts I've had to face is the idea that my hands are now emptied of the other children who I believed should be in their care. And somehow my empty hands result in an empty feeling in my heart. Have you experienced that feeling of emptiness?

Let's not be afraid to answer that question. Instead, let's answer it in the presence of our loving God. Run to him. Answer with the words of our verse this week: "How long must I wrestle with my thoughts and day after day have sorrow in my heart?" (Psalm 13:2). Tell him about your feelings of emptiness. Trust that your Savior will fill you back up to the point of overflowing. God the Father emptied his hands of his one and only Son—willingly! He did that to make us all his own dear children. He wipes away our tears. He comforts us. And he promises us that, through his Son, our hands will embrace our loved ones again in heaven!

While we are still on this earth, let's not forget the other blessings that God has put into our hands. Let's not forget that God might empty our hands because he needs them to fulfill another task that serves his kingdom. Let's also not forget that God often empties our hands only to fill us with an even greater gift—the knowledge that our loved ones are now safely in his arms. When I'm struggling with feelings of emptiness, I focus on this glimpse of heaven:

> *"They are before the throne of God and serve
> him day and night in his temple; and he who
> sits on the throne will shelter them with his pres-
> ence. 'Never again will they hunger; never again
> will they thirst. The sun will not beat down on
> them,' nor any scorching heat. For the Lamb at
> the center of the throne will be their shepherd;
> 'he will lead them to springs of living water.'
> 'And God will wipe away every tear from their
> eyes'" (Revelation 7:15-17).*

These verses are a beautiful reminder of the comfort and perfection that belong to our loved ones in heaven. If my hands were
not meant to wipe away the tears, surely my heart rejoices to know
that God's hands have already dried the very last one.

Prayer: *Dear heavenly Father, forgive me for the times when my
feelings of emptiness cloud my ability to see the rich blessings you've
given me. I praise you for emptying your hands to send me a Savior.
Fill me with your love, your grace, and the knowledge that your
almighty hands will wipe away my tears. Amen.*

☐ **Reflect:** In what ways do you feel empty hands or an empty
heart? For example, what help or care did your hands offer before
your loss? With your hands folded in prayer, run to your heavenly
Father and tell him of your hurts.

■ **Release:** God still has an earthly purpose for your hands—a unique purpose that he has chosen you to fill. How might he use you today? Think of one way to reach out—literally—with your God-given hands today.

DAY 4 Wandering Eyes

After your loss, did you find yourself looking differently at others who still had what you lost? If you lost a spouse, did your eyes suddenly notice all of the couples around you? If you lost a child, did your eyes find moms or dads who still had their children or moms who were still expecting? Did you look differently at a parent holding his or her infant or pushing a little one in a stroller?

As your eyes wandered, did your thoughts wander as well? I know I'm guilty of this one. It upset me to listen to a pregnant woman complain about the size of her belly or how much the baby was kicking. *At least that baby is healthy and growing,* I would think. *Be grateful for what you have.* Does it frustrate you to hear a mom or dad talk about their struggles with their living children? Perhaps you think, *Yes, but at least they're still here with you.* Oh, how Satan loves to play with our minds!

Our theme verse for this week, Psalm 13:2, ends with this question, "How long will my enemy triumph over me?" How long will Satan play to our jealous, coveting, ungrateful natures? As long as he can. He wants your eyes to wander. He wants your eyes on the things you don't have. He wants your eyes to search in discontentment. Just say no! Let's read Hebrews 12:1-3 as we address the temptation of wandering eyes:

> *Since we are surrounded by such a great cloud of witnesses, let us throw off everything that hinders and the sin that so easily entangles. And let us run with perseverance the race marked out for us, fixing our eyes on Jesus, the pioneer and perfecter of faith. For the joy set before him he endured the cross, scorning its shame, and sat down at the right hand of the throne of God. Consider him who endured such opposition*

> *from sinners, so that you will not grow weary*
> *and lose heart.*

It's clear that these verses are meant to guide us through difficult times—when Satan believes he has the perfect opportunity to strike, when our defenses are down, when we grow weary and lose heart. Even when Satan tries to tangle our feet in the mess of grief, let's run the race that God has for us! When Satan catches our eye with earthly comparisons and seduces us with jealousy, let's fix our eyes on our awesome Savior! It is through this perseverance and focus that God develops our faith and sustains us!

Prayer: *Dear Father in heaven, forgive me for my wandering eyes. In my sinfulness, I covet, judge, and lose sight of you. I deserve your punishment for these sins. Be merciful to me, and remind me that I am at peace with you through Jesus Christ! Amen.*

Reflect: Have you noticed your eyes wandering toward people who still have what you lost? Be honest about what goes through your mind during those moments.

Release: Now that you have identified these wayward thoughts, label them as unproductive. Think instead of how you can replace those thoughts with thoughts of gratitude. How can you encourage others and help them protect their earthly blessings?

DAY 5 How Dare You, Satan!

Satan loves your grief. He wants to mess with your thinking, your relationships, and your view of the future. He wants you to engage in earthly comparisons and impatiently ask, "How long will my enemy triumph over me?" (Psalm 13:2). Most of all, he's hoping that your circumstances will drive you away from God. Do you remember the Old Testament story of Job? Here's what happened:

> One day the angels came to present themselves before the LORD, and Satan also came with them. The LORD said to Satan, "Where have you come from?"
>
> Satan answered the LORD, "From roaming throughout the earth, going back and forth on it."
>
> Then the LORD said to Satan, "Have you considered my servant Job? There is no one on earth like him; he is blameless and upright, a man who fears God and shuns evil."
>
> "Does Job fear God for nothing?" Satan replied. "Have you not put a hedge around him and his household and everything he has? You have blessed the work of his hands, so that his flocks and herds are spread throughout the land. But now stretch out your hand and strike everything he has, and he will surely curse you to your face."
>
> The LORD said to Satan, "Very well, then, everything he has is in your power, but on the man himself do not lay a finger."

> *Then Satan went out from the presence of*
> *the Lord. (Job 1:6-12)*

So it began. Satan was thrilled that he had this opportunity to attack Job's faith. He's thrilled that he has this opportunity to attack yours. Be on the lookout for Satan. He prowls near, waiting to catch you in a moment of weakness. Doesn't that make you angry? I remember yelling, "How dare you, Satan! How dare you think that this will turn me away from my God!"

When Satan does tempt us with adversity, let's take our cue from Job's reaction to losing his family members:

> *At this, Job got up and tore his robe and shaved*
> *his head. Then he fell to the ground in worship*
> *and said: "Naked I came from my mother's*
> *womb, and naked I will depart. The Lord gave*
> *and the Lord has taken away; may the name of*
> *the Lord be praised." In all this, Job did not sin*
> *by charging God with wrongdoing. (Job 1:20-22)*

The Lord gives, and the Lord takes away. We cannot comprehend what God has in mind through it all, but we can respond in awe, humility, and trust: "May the name of the Lord be praised!" Satan plugs his ears when you say or think those words, so scream them at the top of your lungs!

Prayer: *Dear Lord, you are the one who gives and the one who takes away, all for a purpose that is far beyond my comprehension. May your name be praised! Amen.*

■ **Reflect:** Has Satan been attacking you through your grief? How have you seen or felt the effects of this attack?

■ **Release:** Let your conversations today be filled with the words "May the name of the Lord be praised!" Think of someone to whom you can offer these words of childlike faith and trust. Perhaps this experience will bring you comfort as well.

DAY 6 Back to the Future

You remember the movie *Back to the Future,* right? If you ever saw it, you won't forget the performance of actor Michael J. Fox. His mannerisms were perfect! That movie was highly influential in my life, as it forced me to grapple with the concept of a flux capacitor and got "The Power of Love" by Huey Lewis & The News stuck in my head for nearly a decade!

However, I had a major problem with this film. Traveling back in time in a DeLorean sounded exciting at first, until I realized that I could be stuck there indefinitely. Immediately, I felt trapped, like I was experiencing some kind of time-related claustrophobia.

Do you ever feel like your thoughts and attention are forever trapped in the days of your loss? David, our psalmist, certainly did! Have you noticed how many times we've encountered the phrase *how long*? Part of the purpose for our journey together is to break free from this mind-set of captivity. But in order to do that, we need to truly start at the beginning of our journey. So, painful as it may be, go back in time to the days surrounding your loss and spend some time there today. Wrestle with God if you need to. Shed the tears. Ask why. And then celebrate.

Celebrate? Yes. Celebrate the fact that you don't need to be stuck there indefinitely. If we go back in time even further, we see our gracious Father experiencing his own child loss as he watched his only Son die an innocent death on the cross. For you! For me! For our loved ones! Jesus' death didn't leave us with an indefinite ending, though. No! On the third day, he came back to life and sealed the future—our future in heaven! Let's read Romans 8:15-21:

> *The Spirit you received does not make you*
> *slaves, so that you live in fear again; rather,*
> *the Spirit you received brought about your*

*adoption to sonship. And by him we cry, "Abba,
Father." The Spirit himself testifies with our
spirit that we are God's children. Now if we are
children, then we are heirs—heirs of God and
co-heirs with Christ, if indeed we share in his
sufferings in order that we may also share in
his glory.*

*I consider that our present sufferings are not
worth comparing with the glory that will
be revealed in us. For the creation waits in
eager expectation for the children of God to
be revealed. For the creation was subjected to
frustration, not by its own choice, but by the
will of the one who subjected it, in hope that the
creation itself will be liberated from its bondage
to decay and brought into the freedom and glory
of the children of God.*

Prayer: *Dear heavenly Father, hold my hand as I look back to the
days when you called my loved one home. Then bring my thoughts
back to the future—the future I have in heaven because of your
willing sacrifice of your only Son. In you alone I find my freedom,
Lord! Amen.*

◾ **Reflect:** You have a seemingly overwhelming task in front
of you today. With the Lord at your side, go back to the earliest
moments of your grief. How is your grief different now than it was
in the beginning?

▨ **Release:** Throughout the rest of your day, focus your thoughts on your future. Ponder God's promises of heaven—the eternal peace and perfection of a beautiful family reunion!

DAY 7 Conclusion of Week 2: I Got This!

Today I'm remembering a comedy skit from a few years ago. It was set up as a game show called *I Got This!* In the scene, three male relatives compete with one another to pay for dinner at a restaurant. The enthusiasm these gentlemen display as they fight to pay the check on behalf of their family is rather endearing. But as the discussion turns to who will cover more significant family expenses, such as financing long-term nursing home care, their behaviors drastically changed to avoidance, apathy, and agitation. It was a humorous spin on how willing or unwilling we are to extend ourselves for others!

As you've struggled with loss, I'm sure that you, like me, haven't always responded to God's challenges by saying, "I got this!" No way. Our psalm verse for this week didn't say, "I got this," either! Perhaps we could say, "I got this!" when the challenges were smaller and the surface of our faith was merely scratched. Events of loss, however, are overwhelming. They can often produce responses of avoidance, apathy, and agitation.

That's where our amazing God steps in and says, "I got this!" Listen as he speaks to you in Isaiah 41:10-13:

> "Do not fear, for I am with you; do not be dismayed, for I am your God.
> I will strengthen you and help you; I will uphold you with my righteous right hand.
> All who rage against you will surely be ashamed and disgraced;
> those who oppose you will be as nothing
>   and perish.
> Though you search for your enemies, you will not find them.
> Those who wage war against you will be as nothing at all.

> *For I am the* LORD *your God who takes hold of*
> *your right hand and says to you, Do not fear;*
> *I will help you."*

When you're feeling overwhelmed by your loss, turn that burden over to God. He's got this! When you can't hold back tears, cry to your God—he's got this! And, most important, when you contemplate your sinful, human nature, know that you have a Savior who didn't shy away from paying the bill. Instead, he stretched out his arms on the cross for you, as if to say, "I got this!"

Prayer: *Dear Lord, I can't carry these burdens alone. Here they are, Lord. Take them. I trust you to strengthen me, uphold me, and help me, for you alone are my God. Amen.*

▨ **Reflect:** Whatever form your grief is taking today, lay it down at the Lord's feet. Tell him all of your worries, fears, and feelings. As you do, remember that your perfect, personal listener holds all things together!

▨ **Release:** When you begin to wonder whether or not you're handling your grief well, remind yourself that it's not your ability to handle it that matters. Hear the words your heavenly Father is saying: "I got this!"

WEEK 3

DAY 1 Pay Attention!

How many times have you spoken these words? Or perhaps in a moment of impatience, how many times have you thought these words? Think of all the tactics teachers have developed to get their students to pay attention! I've witnessed teachers who turned off the lights, silenced their own voices, raised a finger in the air, or yelled something like, "Hey!" or, "Enough!" Regardless of the specific approach, they all demonstrate that the situation was desperate enough that they felt compelled to drastically alter the environment to draw the students back in.

During this week's devotions, we'll be contemplating the next verse of Psalm 13: "Look on me and answer, LORD my God" (v. 3). Perhaps you're reacting to this psalmist's plea the same way that I did: *Wow. That's a pretty bold thing to say to God.* To me, it seemed like the psalmist was saying, "Look at me when I'm talking to you!" Would you feel out of line saying such a thing to God?

Don't. Let's follow the example of the psalmists who boldly put their requests in front of God and who knew that God would listen. "Hear my cry for help" (Psalm 5:2); "Listen to my cry" (Psalm 17:1); "Hear my cry" (Psalm 28:2); "Let your ears be attentive to my cry" (Psalm 130:2); and "Hear, LORD, my cry for mercy" (Psalm 140:6). Come boldly before your Maker!

Notice, though, that the writer of our theme verse for this week ends the statement by addressing the one who would hear his prayers as the "LORD my God." That's respect. That's confidence. That's surrender to one more powerful.

As you continue your healing process, be bold in prayer this week and surrender your will to the One who is all ears. Though you may feel left in the dark at times, he is paying attention!

Prayer: *Dear Lord, through your Son, Jesus, give me courage to come boldly before your throne. I know you will hear me. I know you will answer me according to your great plan for my life. I praise you for your grace and mercy in my life. Amen.*

Reflect: What have you done in your life, productive or not, to get attention from others? Have you felt that God is looking away from you during this time of grief? How has the need for God's . attention manifested itself in your life and in your emotions?

Release: Knowing that God is definitely paying attention to you, what would you like to say? Note how often the psalmists used the word *cry* in their requests for attention. What are the cries of your heart today? Knowing that God is definitely paying attention to you, what would you like him to see in your life today?

DAY 2 Why, Lord?

At the heart of the Christian's grieving process, you'll find this question: *Why, Lord?* I'm sure you've asked that question; I know I have. What's interesting is that this question is usually the result of crisis, grief, trauma, difficulty, pain . . . you get the idea. We don't often ask why when the Lord has blessed us with things we view positively. But in our struggles, we want answers. We want control. We want information. We want to make sense of it all.

Our theme verse for this week shows us David who, in his anguish, cried out for answers too. "Look on me and answer, LORD my God" (v. 3). But in your thoughts and prayers today, consider the fruitlessness of asking why. Isaiah guides us as we think about this:

> *Who has measured the waters in the hollow of his hand, or with the breadth of his hand marked off the heavens? Who has held the dust of the earth in a basket, or weighed the mountains on the scales and the hills in a balance? Who can fathom the Spirit of the LORD, or instruct the LORD as his counselor? Whom did the LORD consult to enlighten him, and who taught him the right way? Who was it that taught him knowledge, or showed him the path of understanding? (Isaiah 40:12-14)*
>
> *Lift up your eyes and look to the heavens: Who created all these? He who brings out the starry host one by one and calls forth each of them by name. Because of his great power and mighty strength, not one of them is missing. Why do you complain, Jacob? Why do you say, Israel, "My way is hidden from the LORD; my cause*

> *is disregarded by my God"? Do you not know?*
> *Have you not heard? The LORD is the everlasting*
> *God, the Creator of the ends of the earth. He will*
> *not grow tired or weary, and his understanding*
> *no one can fathom. (Isaiah 40:26-28)*

These verses help us see that we can ask God why our loss happened as many times as we want, but our sinful minds are unable to comprehend the full answer. What we can do is pray for insight and marvel at our mighty God! I urge you to go back and read the verses again, this time with the realization that the same God who created all things holds you in his hands.

Who are we to deserve such a God! (Now that's cause for asking why!) Love is the answer. "God demonstrates his own love for us in this: While we were still sinners, Christ died for us" (Romans 5:8). God loves you so much that he gave up his only Son for you. God loves you so much that he calls you his child. God loves you so much that he will answer your questions when the time is right.

Prayer: *Dear Father in heaven, forgive my lack of faith in you, which sometimes leads me to question your ways. Remind me always that it is out of your love for me that you draw me close through life's challenges. Amen.*

■ **Reflect:** Does it seem that you have more questions than answers lately? What are the questions that run through your mind most often?

■ **Release:** If possible, spend some time outdoors today— perhaps underneath a sky full of stars. Stand in awe of the God who created such an amazing universe and still knows your every need. In those moments, recognize that God sees far beyond your pain and suffering; his love for you reaches to infinity—beyond the farthest star you can see!

DAY 3 Letting Go

Remember fighting over a toy with your siblings or friends? Picture the scene: two children, each with his clutches on the same toy. A tug-of-war ensues. Grips get tighter, faces get angrier, and voices get louder. Why all the fuss? Each child believes he has a right to the toy. Each child wants control. Each child wants instant gratification. As onlookers, it might be easy for us to say, "It's not worth fighting over. Find something else to play with. Just let go." But do you remember how difficult it was to be the one to let go in the middle of that kind of battle? Somehow it feels like defeat. We've lost something, and our pride is crushed.

We might be tempted to think that we're above fighting for things now that we're adults. Ahem, I beg to differ. How would you describe your "grip" on your life and the things in it? Are you fighting with God over control? Did you catch a hint of the desire for control in our theme verse this week: "Look on me and answer, Lord my God" (Psalm 13:3)?

As a person who likes to feel a sense of control, I easily fall into the trap of believing that somehow if I let go, things will fall apart. Somehow it will be like admitting weakness. And like a child tugging on a toy, I'm afraid I'm going to lose something and my pride will be crushed. To refocus, read the words of 1 Peter 5:5b-7 with me: "'God opposes the proud but shows favor to the humble.' Humble yourselves, therefore, under God's mighty hand, that he may lift you up in due time. Cast all your anxiety on him because he cares for you."

Can't you feel your grip relaxing and the tension of needing control melting away as you read those words? Our lives truly are under God's direction! Let go. Your loved one's life was under God's direction. Let go. God wants to take on your anxieties. Let go. God cares for you. Let go. Through Christ, your future has been won for you; your sins, failures, and shortcomings are now replaced with the perfection of Christ. Let go!

Prayer: *Dear Lord God, forgive me for thinking that I can somehow take control over your will. My times truly are in your hands. Open my heart and my hands; loosen my grip on the things of this world. Help me to trust your timing. Amen.*

■ **Reflect:** What are you holding on to as part of your grief? How does your desire for control display itself in your life? In what way(s) is your desire for control holding you back from fully trusting God?

■ **Release:** What can you do today that will help you remember to let go? Can you think of ways that letting go and trusting the Lord more completely will benefit those around you?

DAY 4 David's Experience With Child Loss: Part 1

Over the next few days, we're going to look at how David experienced child loss and how he responded to it. First, a little background.

The kings and armies, including David's, were off to war. David stayed at his palace in Jerusalem during this time, while he sent Joab with his army to destroy the Ammonites and attack Rabbah. One evening, as David looked out from the palace rooftop, he saw a woman named Bathsheba bathing. Struck by her beauty, David sent for Bathsheba and slept with her. She conceived and sent word to David, telling him that she was pregnant.

David plotted and schemed to cover up this sin. He sent for Uriah, Bathsheba's husband, who was fighting in David's army. David got him drunk, hoping that Uriah would then sleep with Bathsheba and think that the child she would bear was his own. This plan failed. David plotted again, this time to have Uriah put on the front lines of battle, where his death was a certainty. Uriah was killed, and Bathsheba became David's wife. In David's eyes, his plan succeeded. But in 2 Samuel 11:27, we read, "But the thing David had done displeased the LORD."

The Lord sent Nathan to confront David about this sin. After David recognized his guilt and confessed his sins, Nathan said, "The LORD has taken away your sin. You are not going to die. But because by doing this you have shown utter contempt for the LORD, the son born to you will die" (2 Samuel 12:13,14). *To be continued . . .*

I know it's difficult to pause at this point in the plot, but let's take a deep look into those first emotions we experienced after we realized our loved one would not be with us any longer. When I tried to put myself in David's shoes as he listened to this news, I wondered if my thought process might have gone something like this: *Lord, thank you for your forgiveness! I'm not going to die? Thank you for preserving my life, Lord. How gracious! Wait . . . my son . . . Take me! Take me! Spare this little life!* In those moments when he realized what was to come, do you think David felt guilty that his own life was spared? Did you ever wish you had been able to take the place of the one you lost, that he or she might live?

As you contemplate those questions, keep Romans 14:8,9 in mind: "If we live, we live for the Lord; and if we die, we die for the Lord. So, whether we live or die, we belong to the Lord. For this very reason, Christ died and returned to life so that he might be the Lord of both the dead and the living." We are still here. In the Lord, we still have a purpose for being here. So let us focus our energy on living for the Lord while he keeps us here on earth. According to his timing, we will be together again with our loved ones in heaven. Until then, these verses remind us that we are united with our loved ones under Christ, Lord of both the dead and the living!

Prayer: *Heavenly Father, thank you for sending your Son to wash my sins away and give me the gift of eternal life. Help me live my life for you, knowing that you still have a purpose and a calling for my life. Amen.*

■ **Reflect:** How did you respond to the account of David in this devotion? How would you have reacted to the news David received as a result of his sin? How did his reaction compare with your reaction to your recent loss?

◼ **Release:** How might God still use you for his kingdom work? Who in your life needs to hear about Jesus? How might your grief story be a way to share Jesus with that person?

DAY 5 David's Experience With Child Loss: Part 2

We ended our last visit talking about the news Nathan gave David, that the son born to him and Bathsheba would die. The story continues like this:

> *After Nathan had gone home, the Lord struck the child that Uriah's wife had borne to David, and he became ill. David pleaded with God for the child. He fasted and spent the nights lying in sackcloth on the ground. The elders of his household stood beside him to get him up from the ground, but he refused, and he would not eat any food with them. (2 Samuel 12:15-17)*

When I first read these verses, the sentence that really hit me was this: "David pleaded with God for the child." Wow, do I remember those moments with God. To plead with someone is to cry out to them, beg them, and offer arguments and emotional appeals. In David's case, he was pleading even after God's decision had been made. When the outcome of our pleading ends up being different than we had hoped, it may seem that God is against us. But after your loved one's final heartbeat, was God really against you?

Consider this question while we echo the psalmist's words: "Look on me and answer, LORD my God" (13:3). Have you suffered this loss because God was acting against you? Heavens, no! When you're looking to God for answers, know that he is for you. Know that he loves you!

Dear child of God, rejoice in the Lord's great love for you! When we are preoccupied with pain and pleading, it's easy to forget that the Lord works all things out for our *eternal* good, not simply for our earthly good. Know also that as you plead, Jesus is also pleading for you. Though you know that, like David, you are guilty of sin and deserve eternal death in hell, you also know that

God's only Son came to earth for you. He died on the cross and rose again to plead your case before the throne of God! Through Jesus, we are declared innocent. The victory has been won!

Prayer: *Dear Savior, thank you for pleading my case even as you pleaded the case of my loved one who now is with you in heaven. In those moments when I recall how I pleaded with you for my loved one's earthly life, remind me of your earthly life, death, and resurrection! Amen.*

▨ **Reflect:** Did you find yourself pleading with God when you lost your loved one? During your first moments of loss, did you ever feel that God was acting against you?

▨ **Release:** Are there times when it is difficult for you to remember that God acts on your behalf in an eternal way? Describe what makes those moments so difficult, and pray for God to help you keep his eternal perspective in mind when you experience those moments again. Be patient with the grieving process today, and remind yourself to think beyond this temporal, earthly life. Your God certainly does!

DAY 6 David's Experience With Child Loss: Part 3

David pleaded with God. Yet on the seventh day, David lost his son. David was not aware of the death right away, but his servants knew. They were afraid to tell David the news out of fear that he might do something desperate. Read what happened next in 2 Samuel 12:19,20:

> David noticed that his servants were whispering among themselves, and he realized the child was dead. "Is the child dead?" he asked. "Yes," they replied, "he is dead." Then David got up from the ground. After he had washed, put on lotions and changed his clothes, he went into the house of the Lord and worshiped. Then he went to his own house, and at his request they served him food, and he ate.

Does David's thinking seem a little backwards to you? Wouldn't you think the news of his son's death would cause David to stay on the ground even longer? Forget hygiene, lotion, and fashion! Forget going out of the house! And, good grief, forget food!

David's actions, as told in these verses, represent a turning point. His actions speak of acceptance. They speak of being active in the Lord. And they speak of being so confident in the Lord's bidding that David was relaxed enough to eat.

Perhaps you have reached this point of acceptance. Perhaps you haven't. Perhaps you are able to put on an attitude of acceptance toward God's will and are ready to respond to his call of action. Maybe you are still struggling. Let's follow David into the house of the Lord and worship! In God's great wisdom, your loved one is at peace in heaven. And, in God's great wisdom, you are still here as an instrument of that peace for others around you!

Prayer: *Dear Lord, forgive me for the times I stay on the ground in my grief. Fill me with the news of your innocent suffering, death, and resurrection! Use me as an instrument of your peace, Lord! Amen.*

▧ **Reflect:** How have you "stayed on the ground" during your grief so far? Have you tried to hide away? Who might be missing out on time with you as a result? As you have read the account of David's pleading and his grief, what have you found to be especially encouraging?

▧ **Release:** In a spirit of acceptance, do something today that moves you toward a turning point in the grieving process. Try something that you've been reluctant to do since your loved one passed away.

DAY 7 David's Experience With Child Loss: Part 4

Today marks the end of our time with David. During our last visit, we questioned David's response to the news that his child was dead. We were not alone in asking those questions! Check out the reaction from David's servants: "His attendants asked him, 'Why are you acting this way? While the child was alive, you fasted and wept, but now that the child is dead, you get up and eat!'" (2 Samuel 12:21).

Okay, David, let's have it! What were you thinking? Here's what David said: "While the child was still alive, I fasted and wept. I thought, 'Who knows? The LORD may be gracious to me and let the child live.' But now that he is dead, why should I go on fasting? Can I bring him back again? I will go to him, but he will not return to me" (2 Samuel 12:22,23).

That's a pretty solid defense, wouldn't you say? It's interesting that David associated God's graciousness with keeping his son alive. Perhaps we had the same reaction—that God's graciousness would mean blessing us with more time on earth with our loved ones. While we can't bring our loved one back, we can get a better understanding of God's graciousness in our lives.

God graciously sent Jesus to this earth to live perfectly for us. God graciously offered Jesus' life for us, sinners though we are. Jesus graciously conquered death for us. Because of God's grace, we can now confidently say with David, "I will go to him!" We will! It's a certainty!

Prayer: *Dear heavenly Father, thank you for the promise of heaven that we have through your Son, Jesus! Thank you for your graciousness in my life on earth and the eternal life I await in heaven! Amen.*

Reflect: Would you agree with David's definition of God's graciousness—that keeping your loved one alive would have been the gracious thing to do? In what ways was your loved one's passing a gracious act of God?

Release: Thinking of today's devotion, write a new definition—your own definition—of God's graciousness in your life. List ways God has been gracious to you.

WEEK 4

DAY 1 Give Light to My Eyes, or I Will Sleep in Death

Last week, we echoed the psalmist's request for answers: "Look on me and answer, LORD my God" (13:3). We wrestled with the idea that we, as sinful human beings, won't ever be able to fully comprehend God's plan. We witnessed David's experience with child loss and his response to God's will. This week, we continue searching, voicing the plea of Psalm 13: "Give light to my eyes, or I will sleep in death" (v. 3).

When was the last time your eyes craved light? Perhaps you have lived through a power outage recently. Or maybe you had to search for something while the light was off. Perhaps a light burned out at the most inopportune time. Whatever the situation, we can all relate to the frustration of being left in the dark. When crisis strikes, we may feel that we have been left in the dark with respect to God's will. We end up thinking, *Show me what this means for my life, Lord. Reveal the lesson I'm supposed to learn from this experience.*

The theme for our devotions this week takes us deeper in our search for light than mere frustration, though, doesn't it? It sounds desperate and impatient. Perhaps you have reached this point emotionally while waiting for God to reveal his will and purpose. If you have, you may be tempted to run! You may be tempted to trust in your own devices, your own private means of control. While that may feel productive at the moment, in the end, you'll only find yourself farther from the light than when you began.

Cling to the One who offers us the light of life, which is far greater than light that reveals the answers only to our earthly questions! Jesus said, "I am the light of the world. Whoever follows me will never walk in darkness, but will have the light of life" (John 8:12). Be patient. Follow as he leads. Be still in his promises.

In Isaiah chapter 60, God speaks to the penetrating darkness of sin that covers all humanity. Read about how God promised to bring his people out of darkness and sorrow into the light of his salvation:

> "Arise, shine, for your light has come,
> and the glory of the Lord rises upon you.
>
> See, darkness covers the earth
> and thick darkness is over the peoples,
> but the LORD rises upon you
> and his glory appears over you.
>
> Nations will come to your light,
> and kings to the brightness of your dawn.
>
> Lift up your eyes and look about you:
> All assemble and come to you;
> your sons come from afar,
> and your daughters are carried on the hip.
>
> Then you will look and be radiant,
> your heart will throb and swell with joy;
> the wealth on the seas will be brought to you,
> to you the riches of the nations will come.
>
> The sun will no more be your light by day,
> nor will the brightness of the moon shine on you,

for the Lord will be your everlasting light,
and your God will be your glory.

Your sun will never set again,
and your moon will wane no more;
the LORD will be your everlasting light,
and your days of sorrow will end.

Then all your people will be righteous
and they will possess the land forever.
They are the shoot I have planted,
the work of my hands,
for the display of my splendor.

The least of you will become a thousand,
the smallest a mighty nation.
I am the LORD;
in its time I will do this swiftly."
(Isaiah 60:1-5,19-22)

What an amazing picture of hope God gives us—of life in the perfect light of his salvation. For a time, you may feel like you're in the dark, but trust that God's light will shine—forever. Revel in his eternal purpose for you. Because of your Savior Jesus Christ, your sins are forgiven and you will see the light of heaven!

Prayer: *Dear heavenly Father, today I pray for your forgiveness and mercy. How I long for the light of heaven! Teach me patience and renew my faith in you. In the name of your Son, Jesus, I pray. Amen.*

■ **Reflect:** What aspects of your grief make you feel as though you are still in darkness? What answers have you received or lessons have you learned that are bringing light to your world?

■ **Release:** Find a special way to appreciate light today. Go for a walk in the sunshine or light a candle during dinner. Add a unique outdoor light to your garden. Whatever you choose to do, let the source of that light remind you of the hope you have in Christ!

DAY 2 Broken

There came a point in my grieving process when I was finally broken. It was awesome. If I were to characterize what was going on in my heart at that time, I would say it had surrendered the desire for control, loosened its grip, and left its stubborn ways behind. It had taken an emotional blow and had been crushed, melted by the tears that followed and purified of its stigmas and stereotypes. In those moments, I suddenly felt ready. Ready for what? I wasn't exactly sure, but I felt a greater willingness to follow wherever God would lead. I was filled with an increased sense of empathy for others. I felt more connected to the people around me, stranger or not. I was broken! It was the kind of enlightenment that our psalmist pleads for in our verse for the week: "Give light to my eyes, or I will sleep in death" (13:3). In one fell swoop, the words of Psalm 34:17-19 echoed my story: "The righteous cry out, and the LORD hears them; he delivers them from all their troubles. The LORD is close to the broken-hearted and saves those who are crushed in spirit. The righteous person may have many troubles, but the LORD delivers him from them all."

I cried and was heard. I was troubled and delivered. I was brokenhearted and crushed, but the Lord saved me. But these words in Psalm 34 aren't just for me. They're for you as well! Through any trial, God wants to refine our hearts. He doesn't refine them just for kicks, either. Refining happens for a purpose, his purpose. You might see yourself as broken, but God sees you as just about ready!

You are God's child. You have been redeemed by his Son. You are now caught up in the identity of a perfect and holy God, a God whose hands are upon your heart. God drew you from your darkness into his light! With that in mind, read Isaiah 61:1-3 and see what your Savior has accomplished for you.

> *The Spirit of the Sovereign* LORD *is on me,*
> *because the* LORD *has anointed me*
> *to proclaim good news to the poor.*
> *He has sent me to bind up the brokenhearted,*
> *to proclaim freedom for the captives*
> *and release from darkness for the prisoners,*
> *to proclaim the year of the* LORD's *favor*
> *and the day of vengeance of our God,*
> *to comfort all who mourn,*
> *and provide for those who grieve in Zion—*
> *to bestow on them a crown of beauty instead*
>   *of ashes,*
> *the oil of joy*
> *instead of mourning,*
> *and a garment of praise*
> *instead of a spirit of despair.*
> *They will be called oaks of righteousness,*
> *a planting of the* LORD
> *for the display of his splendor.*

Though you have been brokenhearted, captive, and a prisoner in darkness, find your freedom in the light of Jesus. Though you have been covered with ashes, the oil of mourning, and a spirit of despair, look to the one who gives you a crown of beauty, the oil of gladness, and a garment of praise. Though you have been broken, you are now made whole in and for the glory of God!

Prayer: *Dearest Lord, thank you for showing me, through this process, how much you love me. Thank you for declaring me free from sin and darkness! Remind me that my feelings of brokenness are a new beginning. Lead me, Lord! Amen.*

■ **Reflect:** Describe your current level of brokenness. In what ways have you felt yourself surrendering to the grieving process? In what ways are you still clinging to your sense of control in this life?

■ **Release:** If you can relate to the newfound empathy and sense of connectedness that results from being broken, how can you use that empathy to comfort someone else today? Find a way to use this God-given refinement to benefit those around you.

DAY 3 Beating the Body

When was the last time you trained for a physical competition? Do you remember your body feeling *well used?* In 1 Corinthians, Paul talks about an athlete's training approach leading up to the big competition. Let's take a look at what Paul says about the worth of strict training in 1 Corinthians 9:25-27:

> *Everyone who competes in the games goes into strict training. They do it to get a crown that will not last, but we do it to get a crown that will last forever. Therefore I do not run like someone running aimlessly; I do not fight like a boxer beating the air. No, I strike a blow to my body and make it my slave so that after I have preached to others, I myself will not be disqualified for the prize.*

Paul talks about two categories of people—those who pursue a temporary prize through physical competition and those who pursue an eternal prize. Interestingly, we may fit into both categories of people. We may train for physical competitions and receive a "crown" that will not last. But we're also redeemed children of God who will receive a heavenly crown that will last forever! It's this eternal crown of hope that gives us our purpose and direction.

Paul uses this racing analogy to show us that, like a competitive runner in strict training, we should expect hardship, struggles, and challenges in this life. While the competitive runner may face a tough workout, the spiritual runner faces a test of his or her faith. While the competitive runner may have to fight temptations to slack off on the training or to indulge in unhealthy foods, the spiritual runner has to steer clear of the desires and temptations of this world.

So when was the last time you engaged in spiritual training? (Perhaps that should have been my opening question!) Paul's words encourage you to sharpen your focus as you push your way through your time of grief. Compete! Train! Pursue the crown! Though you've been through a difficult, emotional workout during your loss, remember that an eternal crown awaits you.

Prayer: *Dear heavenly Father, be with me as I train spiritually. Guide me, shape me, and lead me to the finish line. Fill me with faithfulness for this journey, Lord. Amen.*

■ **Reflect:** How can you compare your grieving process so far to a physical workout? Take some time to identify moments that have been more exhausting or required more exertion than others.

■ **Release:** If you are able, do something physical today. Allow your increased heart rate, heavier breathing, and tiring muscles to symbolize your spiritual journey during this time of grief.

DAY 4 Running Uphill

My typical running route ends with a climb. It's not an incredibly difficult hill, but it's a hill nonetheless. And by the end of a long run, it's almost as if my legs can feel it coming. Ugh, ugh, and up we go. It always amazes me that the final climb of my runs somehow manages to feel like it takes forever, like I'm running in slow motion. While working my way up the hill, I push myself with thoughts like, *Just imagine when you've made it up the hill . . . that will feel so great! Feel the ice-cold water refreshing your whole body as you drink it.* And, *How great it will be to take a shower!* It's as though my craving for the future gets me through the present.

At the end of my last run, I realized how much that uphill climb has in common with a time of grief. We feel like our grief will never end. We feel as though life is moving in slow motion. We long for the day when our mourning is over, when we enjoy a sense of normalcy again. We want to wash away the trials of the past and experience refreshment and renewal.

Because of the greatness of our amazing God, you have the victor's crown—the gift of heaven—at the end of your run on earth. Jesus, your living water, quenches your thirst and renews your soul day by day. He gave his life for you. He conquered the grave—he conquered the grave for your loved one. He waits for you in heaven at the end of your climb! Our craving for this perfect future refreshment keeps us connected to Christ and gets us through the present.

Think of the way Jesus described this to the woman who came to the well in Samaria.

> "If you knew the gift of God and who it is that asks you for a drink, you would have asked him and he would have given you living water."

> "Sir," the woman said, "you have nothing to draw with and the well is deep. Where can you

> *get this living water? Are you greater than our*
> *father Jacob, who gave us the well and drank*
> *from it himself, as did also his sons and his*
> *livestock?"*

> *Jesus answered, "Everyone who drinks this*
> *water will be thirsty again, but whoever drinks*
> *the water I give them will never thirst. Indeed,*
> *the water I give them will become in them a*
> *spring of water welling up to eternal life."*
> *(John 4:10-14)*

That living water of eternal life through Jesus' love is for you too! Praise the Lord! Drink deeply!

Prayer: *Dear living water, I praise and thank you for the refreshment and renewal that you provide for me every day. How I long to be with you in heaven! While I am here, guide my footsteps and wash over me with your grace and mercy. Amen.*

■ **Reflect:** How would you describe your current position in the uphill climb of grief? What is your sense of how far you've come and how far you have yet to go?

■ **Release:** Schedule a walk with a family member or friend. Pay attention to the hills and valleys that come along during your walk, and pay attention to how you feel when you enjoy a refreshing drink of water afterward!

DAY 5 Chains to Advance the Gospel

Today I'm going to share with you one of the greatest lessons I've learned as I have grieved. God doesn't use suffering and grief to change only what's inside us individually, but he uses them to change what is around us as well! Let me explain.

While studying the book of Philippians, I came to the section that in my Bible is titled "Paul's Chains Advance the Gospel." Intrigued, I read the following words that Paul wrote while in prison:

> Now I want you to know, brothers and sisters,
> that what has happened to me has actually
> served to advance the gospel. As a result, it has
> become clear throughout the whole palace guard
> and to everyone else that I am in chains for
> Christ. And because of my chains, most of the
> brothers and sisters have become confident in
> the Lord and dare all the more to proclaim the
> gospel without fear. (Philippians 1:12-14)

Until I read these verses, I hadn't considered that my earthly struggles could help advance the gospel. In fact, I would've said that I tried to keep my earthly struggles to myself as I pushed forward with the biggest smile I could muster. (Remember the isolation of pain?) But Paul's example turned the light on for me: I am not the only one who faces the spiritual or emotional struggles of grief. And because I'm not the only one, I have an opportunity to witness my faith through the "chains" in my life. What a moment of light for my eyes! (See Psalm 13:3.)

So it was through Paul's chains that I was moved to open my mouth. As he said, because of his chains, "most of the brothers and sisters have become confident in the Lord and dare all the more to proclaim the gospel without fear" (v. 14). So what does this mean for you?

God hasn't used your grief to only change you on the inside; he knows there will be a larger return on his investment! He knew the spiritual and emotional journey you'd endure. But he also knew that with his strength you could survive your loss. And he knew you'd be a witness for your faith through it all. Through Christ, your chains will advance the gospel. So don't hesitate to let everyone know that you've been "in chains for Christ" so that they will be encouraged by the gospel and encouraged to share the gospel message as well.

Prayer: *Dear Lord, help me realize that my earthly struggles are not used only for my eternal good, but they can also benefit those around me. Open my eyes to see others who might be grieving, and fill me with the courage to testify to your grace and mercy! Amen.*

Reflect: How might God use your life as a showcase for his love, compassion, and salvation? Who are the people in your life who need the gospel, and who might be reached through your personal message of hope in times of trouble?

Release: Explore your local community and church for a grief support group or ministry. Are there ways you could participate in such a group and, as you do, witness your faith? If no support groups exist, would you consider starting one?

DAY 6 Naomi's Experience With Loss: Part 1

For the next two days, we're going to look at the Old Testament woman named Naomi. During a time of famine, Naomi, her husband Elimelech, and her two sons and their wives all traveled to the land of Moab hoping that life would be better there. But Naomi's husband died shortly thereafter. Her sons both married Moabite women (Ruth and Orpah), but about ten years later, the sons also died.

After experiencing these losses, this is what Naomi said to Ruth and Orpah: "It is more bitter for me than for you, because the LORD's hand has turned against me!" (Ruth 1:13). Later she said, "Don't call me Naomi [Naomi means *pleasant*]. Call me Mara [Mara means *bitter*], because the Almighty has made my life very bitter. I went away full, but the LORD has brought me back empty. Why call me Naomi? The LORD has afflicted me; the Almighty has brought misfortune upon me" (Ruth 1:20,21).

It's easy for us to empathize with Naomi; we remember, or perhaps still experience from time to time, the feelings of bitterness and affliction that came with our losses. Our lives might very well have been full before the loss happened, but now we feel emptiness.

How do you think God viewed Naomi's situation? How do you think God views your situation now? Is loss meant to be an affliction or to bring misfortune upon us? Truthfully, it may feel that way at the time, but read the following from Hebrews 12:18,19,22-24:

> You have not come to a mountain that can be
> touched and that is burning with fire; to dark-
> ness, gloom and storm; to a trumpet blast or
> to such a voice speaking words that those who
> heard it begged that no further word be spoken
> to them. . . . But you have come to Mount

*Zion, to the city of the living God, the heavenly
Jerusalem. You have come to thousands upon
thousands of angels in joyful assembly, to the
church of the firstborn, whose names are written
in heaven. You have come to God, the Judge of
all, to the spirits of the righteous made perfect, to Jesus the mediator of a new covenant,
and to the sprinkled blood that speaks a better
word than the blood of Abel.*

As we face our sufferings and trials, the Lord draws us to his Word, where he gives us a glimpse of his glory and of the glory that he gives to his church—his believers. We haven't come to a place of darkness and gloom but a place of the light and hope of heaven! God called to Naomi through her suffering, and he does the same for you. Seek him in his Word. Rest in his promises. Remember that you are among those whose names are written in heaven!

Prayer: *Dear Lord, help me recognize your hand at work in my life, and help me remember that you work all things for my eternal good. Amen.*

Reflect: Take a few moments to think about how your loving God views this time of grief for you. Imagine him closely watching your life as your champion and advocate. While you reflect, remind yourself that God has hopes, plans, and purposes for you beyond what you can see or imagine. Describe what it's like to know that your God pays such close attention to you.

■ **Release:** Think of the care and attention that God has for you. Apply that same care and attention toward someone else in your life today. Let the people closest to you know that you are proud of them, that you pray for them, or that you are thinking of them today.

DAY 7 Naomi's Experience With Loss: Part 2

As Naomi grieved the loss of her husband and two sons, she urged her daughters-in-law, Ruth and Orpah, to leave her and find new husbands. Reluctantly, Orpah said goodbye; but Ruth was determined to stay by Naomi's side. Ruth and Naomi traveled to Bethlehem, where Ruth eventually married their next of kin, Boaz. This marriage was significant for many reasons, but one that was important for Naomi is that it meant that her family line would be carried on, leaving her empty no more. Let's read Ruth 4:13-17:

> Boaz took Ruth and she became his wife.
> When he made love to her, the LORD enabled
> her to conceive, and she gave birth to a
> son. The women said to Naomi: "Praise be to
> the LORD, who this day has not left you without
> a guardian-redeemer. May he become famous
> throughout Israel! He will renew your life and
> sustain you in your old age. For your daughter-
> in-law, who loves you and who is better to you
> than seven sons, has given him birth." Then
> Naomi took the child in her arms and cared for
> him. The women living there said, "Naomi has
> a son!" And they named him Obed. He was the
> father of Jesse, the father of David.

Through the marriage of Ruth and Boaz, Naomi now had a grandchild who would be a direct ancestor to our Savior! What amazing blessings! In Naomi's grief, it had been hard for her to imagine the greater purpose for her suffering. She felt empty and afflicted. In our grief, it's difficult to imagine God's greater purpose in allowing that suffering to enter our lives. We feel empty and afflicted. When those feelings strike, let us remember that Naomi's story didn't end there. God had greater blessings in mind for her. Your story doesn't end there, either. God has greater blessings in mind for you as well, not the least of which is the mansion prepared for you in heaven through our Lord and Savior Jesus Christ!

"I remain confident of this: I will see the goodness of the LORD in the land of the living. Wait for the LORD; be strong and take heart and wait for the LORD" (Psalm 27:13,14).

Prayer: *Dear heavenly Father, like Naomi, I can't always see your greater purpose for my suffering. Lead me to trust in you, confident that I will be with you one day in the land of the living. Amen.*

▓ Reflect: Certainly, Naomi's journey from grief to joy reflects the thought of our theme verse—that of moving from darkness into light. Write a list of the blessings, large or small, that God has graciously given to you during this time of grief.

▓ Release: In the moments when you still find yourself empty and waiting for the blessing and greater purpose of your grief, think of ways you can remind yourself that God will not forget to write the rest of your beautiful story as his dearly loved child.

WEEK5

DAY 1 How Can I Speak?

For week 5, we'll be looking at the next portion of Psalm 13, which reads, "My enemy will say, 'I have overcome him,' and my foes will rejoice when I fall" (v. 4). To understand these words, we may need to take a look at the context in which the psalmist David was speaking. A number of times in his life, David was tormented by enemies. We don't know which time he may have been thinking of when he wrote these words. But in this psalm he voices his distress, confusion, and anxiety. He was pleading for help and for understanding so that he would not give up in despair and his enemies would not prevail.

Applied to our grief process, these words capture the emotions caused by the social stresses that flood over us immediately after the loss. Suddenly, we feel we owe the world an explanation of what happened, but we don't know what to say.

We can come up with many social reasons why our tongues are tied right after a loss. First, our own shock can render us speechless. Second, we fear the uncertainty involved in sharing the news with someone. How will this person respond? Will he or she build me up and reassure me? Will they offer unsolicited advice? Will they react like Job's friends, assuming that I've brought this grief on myself by a sin? Might some even gloat over my misfortune? Am I even ready to talk openly about what happened?

We reflected last week on the importance of using our chains to advance the gospel message. In order to fulfill this mission, we need to be ready to speak. So the focus for this week will be on loosening the tongue and preparing to speak of the loss.

If you're still feeling a bit reserved about using your story as a witnessing opportunity, focus on the gospel message that's at the heart of God's will for your life (both the ups and the downs). Sometimes we unintentionally attach labels—like embarrassment, shame, or fear—to our feelings of grief. But that only hinders us from using our grief to further the gospel. When we are tempted to feel that way, we find encouragement in the following verses:

- *I am not ashamed of the gospel, because it is the power of God that brings salvation to everyone who believes. (Romans 1:16)*

- *Yes, and I will continue to rejoice, for I know that through your prayers and God's provision of the Spirit of Jesus Christ what has happened to me will turn out for my deliverance. I eagerly expect and hope that I will in no way be ashamed, but will have sufficient courage so that now as always Christ will be exalted in my body, whether by life or by death. For to me, to live is Christ and to die is gain. (Philippians 1:18-21)*

- *The Spirit God gave us does not make us timid, but gives us power, love and self-discipline. So do not be ashamed of the testimony about our Lord or of me his prisoner. Rather, join with me in suffering for the gospel, by the power of God. He has saved us and called us to a holy life—not because of*

> *anything we have done but because of his own*
> *purpose and grace. This grace was given us*
> *in Christ Jesus before the beginning of time.*
> *(2 Timothy 1:7-9)*

How can you speak about what happened? Through the power of God and the guidance of the Holy Spirit! Trust the power of the almighty God to work—even in and through your grief. Someone out there who has suffered loss might need the very words that God puts in your heart and on your lips!

Prayer: *Dear Lord, I come before you today and ask for a spirit of power, of love, and of self-discipline. Move me to proclaim the gospel message, the very message that assures me of my home in heaven! Amen.*

▨ Reflect: Identify some of the obstacles that prevent you from sharing your grief story. Are you fearful of others' reactions to you? Do you struggle to find the right words to explain what you've been going through? Push yourself to identify the reasons behind your reluctance to speak and to find a way to work past them.

▨ Release: Since today's devotion focused on loosening your tongue and sharing your story, it's only fitting that we put this into practice for our "Release" today! Offer a word of encouragement to someone you meet today; see if it sparks a conversation and an opportunity to share what God has done in your life—even during this time of grief.

DAY 2 Carrying Around Death

Do you ever feel as though you've been carrying around death ever since your loss? While that may sound like a harsh question, here's what I mean: Do you feel as though people see you for your loss? The loss somehow becomes a label. We wear that label whether we want to or not, and we carry it with us as we interact with others. And the label somehow makes the people around us perform an interpersonal dance: *Should I bring it up? Should I stay silent? What are the right things to say in a situation like this? When will this person (and our relationship) get back to normal?*

Our theme verse for this week acknowledges the social challenges we face when enduring loss, defeat, failure, and other frustrations: "My enemy will say, 'I have overcome him,' and my foes will rejoice when I fall" (Psalm 13:4). We can't erase these relational struggles, because we live in a sinful, imperfect, conflict-filled world. We can, however, reframe what it means to carry around death. Rather than an obstacle to communication, it becomes an opportunity to connect. Take a look at 2 Corinthians 4:10-12: "We always carry around in our body the death of Jesus, so that the life of Jesus may also be revealed in our body. For we who are alive are always being given over to death for Jesus' sake, so that his life may be revealed in our mortal body. So then, death is at work in us, but life is at work in you."

While we carry around death in the sense that we've experienced loss, we carry around a death that has amazing eternal significance. We carry around the death of Jesus. Jesus' death becomes our label; it says, "Redeemed." The verses above state that the purpose of carrying around Jesus' death is so that his life may be revealed in us. We have the opportunity to carry his death—our new label—into our interactions (yes, even the challenging conversations!).

Let's reframe together. Let's acknowledge the label of loss but also look at the conversations that arise because we wear that label as opportunities to share the message of what we've gained from our relationship with Christ!

Prayer: *Dear heavenly Father, forgive me for becoming impatient when well-intentioned support leaves me feeling labeled. As I interact with others, put the message of salvation on my lips. Empower me to share the "redeemed" label that your Son won for me on the cross! Amen.*

▢ **Reflect:** Think of your interactions with others since your loss. What forms of support have been the most helpful to you? What attempts at offering support have unintentionally caused you frustration, resentment, or impatience?

▢ **Release:** What can you learn about comforting others from the way you have been comforted during this time? Are there any words or phrases that have been especially helpful for you? Choose a few key strategies that have benefited you the most, and find a way to record them to use with others in the future.

DAY 3 Grave Dressing

Ugh. A rather heavy title today, eh? Allow me to explain. *Grave dressing* is actually a communication term. (Yep, I'm bringing you to my college classroom today!) It's used to describe the introspective, reflective process that a person goes through as they try to get over a breakup. Specifically, grave dressing is creating a three- or four-sentence summary of "what happened" to end the relationship. It allows the person to handle the awkwardness of having to explain the breakup with a comfortable, near-rehearsed, dignified response. If only our psalmist had such modern methods of navigating social discomfort!

I think the concept of grave dressing can be applied to loss as well. When it comes to loss, grave dressing means developing a brief story of what happened that allows you as much comfort as possible while still satisfying the inevitable questions that come from those around you. Have you gone through the grave dressing phase?

What's awesome for us Christians is that our view doesn't end at the grave! Your grave dressing conversations will be short-lived! Take a look at the evidence: "When the perishable has been clothed with the imperishable, and the mortal with immortality, then the saying that is written will come true: 'Death has been swallowed up in victory'" (1 Corinthians 15:54).

How's that for a grave dressing account? Death has been swallowed up in victory! The victory is mine. The victory is yours! The victory belongs to our loved ones! This is your story!

Prayer: *Dear heavenly Father, thank you for the gift of your Son. Because of him, the account of our losses no longer needs to revolve around the grave! Thank you for declaring victory over death and the grave! Amen.*

■ **Reflect:** Take a moment and write a three- or four-sentence summary of your grief story. What is it like to read those words printed on paper? Did your story include the glorious ending we have through faith? If not, rework your story to include the full picture and purpose of this time of grief in your life.

■ **Release:** Share your revised, written grief story with a trusted family member or friend today. Pay attention to the insights and emotions that occur as part of that sharing experience. This sharing process might also help your family member or friend better understand where you are in your grieving process and how you've attached meaning to your loss.

DAY 4 What Is My Story?

This week, we've been focusing on the challenge of voicing the account of our loss to the world. Today's devotion will take us further than the three or four sentences we crafted for the grave dressing process. We're going to tell a story.

Storytelling is an art form. Throughout his earthly life, Jesus certainly utilized this art in his parables. He recognized the power of a story to connect the unfamiliar to the familiar, to hold the audience's attention, and to illustrate a point in a memorable way.

During today's devotion, put on your storytelling hat and embrace this wonderful art form! To write your story, I'd like you to ponder the following:

- What was my life situation before the loss? What was it like to be me?

- What was the immediate impact of the loss on my life and the lives of those around me?

- What lessons have I learned about myself and my faith because of my loss?

- What has God accomplished in my heart through this loss?

- What opportunities might God have for me now that my faith and my heart have been refined by the loss?

As you reflect and form your answers to these questions, pay careful attention to the chronological sequence of the questions. When you're done, your answers should flow together to create your story. Articulating your story will benefit not only you as you deal with your grief, but it can also benefit those around you. God has accomplished something in you. God's hand has been at work in your life. And now it's time to share. To those who doubt God's presence, you can offer assurance. To those who are dwelling in the early stages of grief, you can offer the example of hope in your own story.

Psalm 40:10 says, "I do not hide your righteousness in my heart; I speak of your faithfulness and your saving help. I do not conceal your love and your faithfulness from the great assembly." Though your grief was and is and will be painful, God was and is and will be faithful. Write your story, and speak of God's faithfulness to you as his own dear child.

Prayer: *Dear Lord, give me the words to tell my story. More important, give me the words to tell the story of your faithfulness. Amen.*

▦ **Reflect:** Record your answers to the questions in our devotion for today. Edit them until the story flows smoothly. Add descriptive words that capture your moods and emotions. Give your characters depth and life. Most important, be brave and honest while you write.

▦ **Release:** Find a special way to treasure what you've written. Frame it on the wall, add it to a scrapbook, or place it among your keepsake items. Offering your story a special physical location in your life means that you'll always be able to look back on your experiences and reflect on what God has done in your heart and life.

DAY 5 | Impression Management

Impression management (another fun communication concept) is the process of influencing and shaping the way others perceive us. People often use the phrase to mean that we manipulate the verbal and nonverbal behaviors we display on the outside to create a positive image of what we're like on the inside. As Shakespeare said, "All the world's a stage, and all the men and women merely players" (*As You Like It,* 2.7.1-2).

This week's theme asks us to ponder the relational challenges that surround us during a time of grief: "My enemy will say, 'I have overcome him,' and my foes will rejoice when I fall" (Psalm 13:4). Part of managing these relational challenges is to manage the impression we make on those around us.

So, what impression have you been creating during your time of grief? How have you been shaping the way others see you? It's common during such a difficult stretch to want to force the smile, mask true emotions, and "keep it together" from the outside. I certainly tried to do that! Those are the behaviors that create the most positive impression, right?

While impression management can benefit us and help us to "save face" in many social situations, it lacks authenticity in those cases. Impression management can tempt us to build walls around ourselves so that no one can see or sense our pain. But if we allow impression management to falsely guide our interactions, we are faced with a difficult question: Did God allow your suffering and guide you through your grief in the hope that you would hide or mask the result? No way!

If you're intent on practicing impression management, then practice with authenticity, for the sake of the gospel. Here's the apostle Paul's example of gospel-minded impression management:

Though I am free and belong to no one, I have made myself a slave to everyone, to win as many as possible. To the Jews I became like a Jew, to win the Jews. To those under the law I became like one under the law (though I myself am not under the law), so as to win those under the law. To those not having the law I became like one not having the law (though I am not free from God's law but am under Christ's law), so as to win those not having the law. To the weak I became weak, to win the weak. I have become all things to all people so that by all possible means I might save some. I do all this for the sake of the gospel, that I may share in its blessings. (1 Corinthians 9:19-23)

As an ambassador for Christ, use the person God created you to be (including what he's done in you during your struggles) to win the souls of the people God has put in your life. So rather than working so hard to shape the "earthly" impression others have of you, focus your efforts on shaping their impression of your awesome God! That's an impression worth making!

Prayer: *Dear heavenly Father, forgive me for the times when I get caught up in managing my impression in the eyes of others. Instead, let them see you. Let them see the grace, mercy, and peace that you offer through the redeeming blood of Jesus! Amen.*

Reflect: Describe the impression you've been striving to uphold during your grieving process. Whose opinions are you most concerned about when you're manipulating your impression? In other words, who are you with when this happens?

▨ **Release:** As you consider whose opinions you're most concerned about, think of a way to reframe your view of these relationships and move to be more authentic in them. How can you
share more openly with them the love of your amazing God?

DAY 6 Tearing Down the Walls

In our last devotion, we discussed the concept of impression management. You're certainly not alone if you plead guilty to trying to manage the impressions others have about you, and you're certainly not alone if you've built some pretty serious walls around you in the process! I've done the same thing, thinking that I was sparing others from having to walk with me in my grief.

Let's look beyond our towering walls and open our eyes to see the people around us who recognize our pain and want to offer support. Galatians 6:2 implores, "Carry each other's burdens, and in this way you will fulfill the law of Christ." Carrying each other's burdens is an act of spiritual love and concern! When we maintain the walls around us, we deny others the opportunity to serve God in this way.

As Christians, we have the privilege of belonging to a family of believers who can and want to help us carry the weight of our burdens. That privilege is ours only through Jesus Christ, the one who carried the burden of all of our sins. Through his innocent suffering and death, we were marked as members of his family.

So no matter how high they are or how long you've spent constructing them, tear down the walls you've built around yourself so that you might take advantage of God's blessing of fellowship.

If someone offers to pray for you, give them something specific to lay before our heavenly Father's throne. If someone offers to prepare a meal for you, graciously accept it. If someone offers you a shoulder to cry on, lean in when you're ready. Your acceptance of these offers brings joy to the hearts of those who want to help.

This is your season for receiving the fullest benefits of Christian fellowship on this earth. Someday soon God will equip you to be the faithful, patient support someone else needs. Wouldn't you encourage someone to let you in to offer help and comfort?

Tear down your walls, knowing that the people around you want to encourage you in the same way!

Prayer: *Dear Lord, help me tear down the walls that I've used to protect myself emotionally. Open my eyes to the people you've put in my life who want to help and support me during this difficult time. Thank you for the blessing of Christian fellowship! Amen.*

▓ Reflect: Who has offered to help or support you during your time of loss? Have you been open to their help, or have you put up walls between yourself and them?

▓ Release: Make contact with someone who has offered to help you or whom you know to be a trusted listener. Celebrate the gift of Christian fellowship that you have in that person!

DAY 7 In Need of a Half-Time Speech?

If you've ever participated in sports, perhaps you remember sitting in the locker room during halftime of a game that was off to a disastrous start. Perhaps you can remember the look in your coach's eyes. Boy, oh boy, do I remember! But I also remember that, somehow, that coach was able to turn things around, frame things positively, and even motivate me to push myself harder than ever. Are you in need of a half-time speech? Do you find yourself with your head in your hands, dwelling on where you've been?

Today we're going to look at a half-time speech Paul wrote in his letter to Timothy. Paul is preparing Timothy as a witness for Christ, one who will stay true to sound doctrine. He warns Timothy about people who will stray from doctrine as they pursue their earthly desires. Though doctrinal disaster looms nearby, Paul turns things around for Timothy, frames things positively, and motivates him to push harder than ever. Paul says, "But you, keep your head in all situations, endure hardship, do the work of an evangelist, discharge all the duties of your ministry" (2 Timothy 4:5). Go get 'em, Timothy!

On the one hand, I feel convicted by Paul's pep talk. I know I don't always keep my head. I know I haven't always had an enduring spirit as I've dealt with hardship. And I know that, in this weakness, I haven't always done the work of an evangelist or been faithful to my ministry. On the other hand, I feel encouraged by Paul's words. It's like the half-time pep talk during that game that started out as a disaster.

As I look at my life, I recognize that my sin has turned me into a weak defender, allowing Satan to run up the score. About the time I think I'm in control during a fast break layup, Satan trips me up and steals the ball. Suddenly, I hear a buzzer that pauses the game, and I see my substitute running onto the court to clean up my mistakes and lead me to a seemingly impossible victory!

Because of my Savior, I have a right relationship with God and am both equipped and empowered to spread the Good News.

This is all true for you as well! Consider Paul's half-time pep talk as you go about your day. Go get'em!

Prayer: *Almighty God, I repent of the times that I let my struggles become an obstacle that kept me from sharing the gospel with others. Thank you for sending your Son as my substitute. Remind me of the right relationship I have with you, encourage me with the words Paul spoke to Timothy, and lead me where you will. Amen.*

▨ **Reflect:** Describe your mood over the past few days. Are you in need of a half-time speech? What aspects of your grief have consumed your attention and kept you from being a faithful servant of the gospel?

▨ **Release:** Imagine yourself taking the newfound energy you'd feel after an inspirational half-time speech and applying it to your day today. Focus on keeping your head, having an enduring spirit, and sharing the good news of the gospel. God has a job for you to do!

WEEK 6

DAY 1 But I Trust in Your Unfailing Love

At long last, we've come to the turning point in Psalm 13. Until now, we've dealt with the shock and the questioning that so often are part of the grieving process. We've contemplated our need for answers. We've explored the challenges that cripple our interactions with others. We've done quite a bit of wrestling, haven't we! So now for the turning point: Our theme for this week forms a beautiful confession. Though the loss and the emotions that have followed the loss haven't been easy to accept, "I trust in your unfailing love" (Psalm 13:5a).

Unfailing love! Did you catch that? God's love hasn't failed you. It's easy to feel that somehow there's a lapse in God's love and attention to your life when it is suddenly filled with pain. But God's love hasn't failed you. It's also easy to doubt that you'll survive the grieving process and feel at peace again. But God's love won't fail you!

Consider the words of Lamentations 3:19-26, 31,32:

> I remember my affliction and my wandering,
> the bitterness and the gall. I well remember
> them, and my soul is downcast within me. Yet
> this I call to mind and therefore I have hope:
> Because of the LORD's great love we are not

> *consumed, for his compassions never fail. They*
> *are new every morning; great is your faithful-*
> *ness. I say to myself, "The Lord is my portion;*
> *therefore I will wait for him." The Lord is good*
> *to those whose hope is in him, to the one who*
> *seeks him; it is good to wait quietly for the*
> *salvation of the Lord. For no one is cast off by*
> *the Lord forever. Though he brings grief, he will*
> *show compassion, so great is his unfailing love.*

Though you will always remember the grief you've experi-enced, God doesn't leave you in that grief! If you skim these verses from Lamentations again, you'll see that God replaces the afflic-tion, wandering, bitterness, and gall with sure hope. He fills your overwhelmed heart with his unfailing compassion—every day. In this sinful world where the unexpected often happens, God is your only constant. He offers the only perfect, unconditional faithfulness there is! Through his only Son, you have the certainty of heaven!

Prayer: *Dear Father in heaven, I'm in awe of your unfailing love and faithfulness in my life. Forgive me for the times when I have forgotten that you're there; your unfailing love reminds me that you are with me. I put my trust in you! Amen.*

■ **Reflect:** Confess to the Lord the times when you felt as though he has failed you during this season of loss. Describe for him the moments when you've felt the most alone during this journey. When you're done, move right to the Release section of this devotion!

■ **Release:** Embrace the spirit of Psalm 13:5a for this week. During your Bible study and your prayer time, surrender your pain, anxiety, fear, and need for control to the unfailing love of your heavenly Father.

DAY 2 Turbulence: Part 1

I hate airplane turbulence—the uncertainty, the stomach flip, the rattling drink carts. I hate all of it. Over years of travel, I've developed a few coping mechanisms that help me survive a turbulent flight. If you hate turbulence as much as I do, perhaps you can try these strategies on your next flight! My first coping mechanism is called the "white-knuckle grip of death" and can easily be applied to the arm rest—or pant leg of the person sitting next to you. Your fingers should be in severe pain by the time you let go; if not, your form is incorrect. My second coping mechanism is the "close your eyes to make it all go away" technique. I always hope that this technique might result in falling asleep only to find that we've landed and arrived at the gate. That dream hasn't come true for me yet. A final technique is to shoot an angry look at my husband (or whoever is seated next to me), as if to imply that the turbulence is somehow his fault. *Can't you fix this?*

As I look back on my own experiences with pregnancy loss, I find that I've applied similar coping mechanisms as I've tried to deal with the aftermath. I've used the "white-knuckle grip of death" to cling to anything that makes me feel some sense of security and certainty. I've used the "close your eyes to make it all go away" technique to try to sneak away from the pain or the grief for a while. And, not at all on purpose, I've left my husband feeling even more helpless than he does when I wish he could make the airplane turbulence disappear. In his love for me, he wants to fix my pain, to make it go away. But all he can really do is ride it out with me.

Does any of this sound familiar to you?

I think the reason many of us hate turbulence—life's turbulence—is that it strips us of our perceived sense of control and replaces it with insecurity and uncertainty. It's the opposite of what our theme verse expresses, that we trust in God's unfailing love. In Psalm 16:1-2, 5-11, the same psalmist who wrote our theme verse redirects our approach to the turbulence that may be upsetting our lives.

> *I lift up my eyes to the mountains—*
> *   where does my help come from?*
> *My help comes from the LORD,*
> *   the Maker of heaven and earth.*
>
> *He will not let your foot slip—*
> *   he who watches over you will not slumber;*
> *indeed, he who watches over Israel*
> *   will neither slumber nor sleep.*
>
> *The LORD watches over you—*
> *   the LORD is your shade at your right hand;*
> *the sun will not harm you by day,*
> *   nor the moon by night.*
>
> *The LORD will keep you from all harm—*
> *   he will watch over your life;*
> *the LORD will watch over your coming and going*
> *   both now and forevermore.*

Did you catch all of the assurances of safety and security? The Lord is at my right hand; no "white-knuckle grip of death" necessary. I have set the Lord before me; I don't need to cower away behind closed eyelids. And I don't need to render my husband or others around me helpless; together, we have the Lord as our refuge, the one who will fill us with joy and the hope of heaven. Now that's the best care in the air!

Prayer: *Dearest heavenly Father, when life's travels leave me feeling overwhelmed and insecure, remind me of the words of Psalm 16. I praise you and thank you for the gift of your Son, and I trust your hand to guide me. Amen.*

▓ **Reflect:** In what ways has your grief been like turbulence? How have you attempted to cope with the insecurity and uncertainty? Who or what is the focus of these attempts?

▓ **Release:** Find a quiet spot to be still for a while. Relish the peacefulness of this quiet spot, and embrace the opportunity to be still! Pay attention to the absence of chaos or turbulence. Pay attention to the calm around you. Use this moment of stillness as a chance to pray and thank God for his constant compassion and unfailing love in your life!

DAY 3 Turbulence: Part 2

While our approach to life's turbulence impacts our personal outlook, it also impacts the outlook of those around us. My eyes were opened to this when my husband and I began traveling with our children. When boarding the plane, my kids searched my face, looking for a positive or negative reaction. When the plane began racing down the runway, they looked to me for confirmation that the plane was *supposed* to do that. And when those bumps occurred along the way, they turned to me for comfort. The turbulence wasn't just about me anymore—I now had an audience.

My strategies for coping with turbulence changed right then and there. Remember the "white-knuckle grip of death"? It relaxed and became a hand that could reach out in love. Remember the closed eyes that tried to make the turbulence disappear? They stayed open and offered a connection point that communicated understanding and comfort. And remember the angry looks that created a sense of helplessness? The anger gave way to compassion.

Perhaps this change in my strategy reflects in a small (and imperfect) way God's compassion for us sinners. My sins had a "white-knuckle grip of death" on me. Jesus washed the guilt of those sins away on the cross and now those nail-pierced hands reach out in love to assure me that I'm in a right relationship with God. My sins closed my eyes to the light of God's Word. Jesus sent his Holy Spirit to open my eyes at my baptism and has calmed my heart by keeping my eyes focused on his marvelous promises ever since. My sins deserve God's angry looks and eternal punishment, but God's anger gave way to compassion through his only Son.

As long as I am on this earth, I will have an audience for the episodes of turbulence in my life. Now, because of God's great love for me, I can testify to God's promises! I can reach out in love, offer my understanding and comfort, and express my compassion.

God's plan of salvation is yours! His love, understanding, and compassion are yours! As you face life's turbulence, I pray that the Lord fills you with the gospel message to the point of overflowing. Turbulence is temporary; God's promises are eternal!

Prayer: *Dear Father, use me as a witness of your promises as I face life's turbulence. Fill me with your love, understanding, and compassion so that I may share your grace with those whose focus remains on the temporary trials of this life. Amen.*

■ **Reflect:** Create a list of the people who make up your audience during this loss. What do you believe each of these people has seen or observed in your reaction to loss?

■ **Release:** Choose someone from the list you just created, and make contact with that person today. Use your conversation to make a positive connection, and allow God to use you as a witness for his grace and faithfulness.

DAY 4 Let the Waters Rise

The inspiration for today's devotion comes from Psalm 32:6,7:

*Let all the faithful pray to you while
   you may be found;
surely the rising of the mighty waters will not
   reach them.
You are my hiding place;
you will protect me from trouble
and surround me with songs of deliverance.*

Picture the godly person referred to in this psalm—when the mighty waters rise but don't reach him. What does your picture look like? Is it literal? Do you picture someone being carried or lifted just high enough above the raging waters that he or she stays dry? In the image in your mind, pay attention to the contrast between the rising mighty waters and the security of being untouchable. In my mind, the contrast involves total distress and chaos on the one hand, with peace, security, and trust on the other. The psalmist refers to God as his hiding place. I love this image. If I have a secure place to hide, why should I fear the rising waters?

As you read those verses again, remember your early moments of loss, when you may have felt that the waters were rising too quickly around you. Then imagine yourself in the hiding place that's described in the psalm. Imagine yourself being held securely in your Father's hands. As I look back on my own experience, I know that I was being held in this way. It was God's protection that empowered me to say, "Okay, Lord. If this is your will, let the waters rise."

When the memories, the grief, the tears, or the social stresses make you feel as though you're sinking, run to your hiding place. Confront your fears with the prayer of the psalmist: "You will protect me from trouble and surround me with songs of deliverance" (32:7).

Prayer: *Dear Lord, let the waters rise if you want them to. I know I'm safe in your hands! Should disaster, danger, or loss threaten me, remind me that my life is yours. I will follow you! Amen.*

▨ **Reflect:** In what ways are you still experiencing rising waters during your time of grief? What about your loss still overwhelms you? Share those issues with your Father in prayer.

▨ **Release:** Say a prayer of thanksgiving for the safe hiding place you have in your Lord and Savior. As you do, think back to how God has led you this far through the floods and rising waters of your grief.

DAY 5 I'll Still Love You, Lord

Have you ever watered down your expressions of love by throwing in reminders of the other person's imperfections? I'll give you a few examples. "Even though you really hurt my feelings, I'll still love you." "Even though you don't deserve it, I'll still love you." "Even though you can't cook, I'll still love you." You can insert your own examples into that scenario. The point is that you're holding on to a piece of the negative while declaring your love.

This week's theme focuses on the phrase "But I trust in your unfailing love" (Psalm 13:5). The word *but* ties this statement to what precedes. Applied to our grieving, it could sound like we are saying, "Even though you've allowed my suffering and hardship, I'll still trust you, Lord." Perhaps it leads us to ask the question, Have you held onto the bitterness of your suffering while declaring your love and trust in God?

If anyone has the right to bring up our flaws while declaring love, it's our heavenly Father. Our sinful ways don't even deserve a statement that begins with the words *even though*. Yet because of Jesus, our Father in heaven looks down on us and tells us that even though we've forsaken him in our sinfulness, "I still love you." He isn't expressing bitterness over our sinfulness. Rather, he is showing us just how much he loves us.

Jesus our Savior won that declaration of love for you! In the bitterness of his suffering on the cross, his heart overflowed with love for you. Romans 5:7,8 sums it up perfectly: "Very rarely will anyone die for a righteous person, though for a good person someone might possibly dare to die. But God demonstrates his own love for us in this: While we were still sinners, Christ died for us."

When you're tempted to use your suffering as a condition, that you love God in spite of your suffering, stop in your tracks. Take a closer look at the psalmist's words. He isn't saying that he loves God in spite of his suffering. He is clearly confessing his faith.

"Yes, I have suffered. But I trust in God." He is speaking in much the same spirit as the apostle Paul when he wrote, "Our light and momentary troubles are achieving for us an eternal glory that far outweighs them all" (2 Corinthians 4:17). Instead of hanging on to the bitterness, consider that your suffering is something for which you can love God. He wants you close. He wants to lead you. He wants to hold you in his arms in this life and the next! Even though you've doubted his ways, he'll still love you!

Prayer: *Dear heavenly Father, forgive me for letting my bitterness tarnish my expression of love for you. Set me free from this sinful thinking, and remind me of your unconditional love in sending Jesus to pay the price for my sins. Amen.*

Reflect: In what ways has bitterness colored the expressions of your love for God? For example, have you been holding back complete trust in his plan for you until he offers you a sign that he's listening to you? Write down any reservations or conditions that come to mind.

Release: Is there a loved one in your life who might need to be reminded of your unconditional love? Connect with that person today and renew your commitment to love him or her as Christ loves you.

DAY 6 Breathe Again

After a period of grief, you'll eventually feel some sense of peace and relief. The burden won't feel so heavy anymore. You might even feel a sense of freedom as you realize how you've been trapped under a thick blanket of grief. It's been hard to see beyond your immediate surroundings and to concentrate through your pain. That blanket of grief has kept you cornered in a place of darkness, leaving you longing for a breath of fresh air.

Much like this blanket of grief, our sins trap us, hold us down, limit our vision, and hold us in a place of darkness. And that's what we deserve. We've earned that spot under the blanket of sin, where there's no room to move and no fresh air to breathe. But God has destroyed the power of sin and darkness through Christ:

> *On this mountain he will destroy*
> *the shroud that enfolds all peoples,*
> *the sheet that covers all nations;*
> *he will swallow up death forever.*
> *The Sovereign LORD will wipe away the tears*
> *from all faces;*
> *he will remove his people's disgrace*
> *from all the earth.*
> *The LORD has spoken.*
> *In that day they will say,*
> *"Surely this is our God;*
> *we trusted in him, and he saved us.*
> *This is the LORD, we trusted in him;*
> *let us rejoice and be glad in his salvation."*
> *(Isaiah 25:7-9)*

Our shroud, the symbol of mourning over death that comes as the wages of sin, has been destroyed! Come out into the fresh air and breathe again. Jesus has won salvation for us and for the ones whom we've lost. And the description of God's work doesn't stop there! Through our Savior Jesus Christ, the horrors of death are swallowed up. The tears and disgrace are gone. Breathe again.

You can count on God's unfailing love for you. The end of Isaiah chapter 25 verse 8 reads, "The LORD has spoken." What greater finality or assurance could you ask for? The One who hung every star in the sky, calms the sea, and tells the sun and moon when to shine is the same One who gives you the personal promise of salvation through Jesus. Because we can count on God's promises, we can confess with Isaiah, "Surely this is our God; we trusted in him, and he saved us. This is the LORD, we trusted in him; let us rejoice and be glad in his salvation" (55:9).

Rejoice in the Lord! He's lifted your blanket of sin, and he'll lift your blanket of grief. Trust in his promises, come out into the fresh air, and breathe again!

Prayer: *Dear Lord, thank you for setting me free from the stifling grip of sin. Set me free from my grief as well, and fill me with trust in your promises. Because of your love, I can breathe again. Amen.*

Reflect: Describe your ability to "breathe again" at this point in your grieving process. How are you experiencing a renewed spirit? In what ways are you still pressed down under your blanket of grief?

Release: Take a few moments to breathe deeply, preferably outdoors if you're able. As you breathe, remind yourself of the peace your Savior won for you and your loved one. Death has no hold on you or your loved one; breathe in your freedom!

DAY 7 Spoken For

If you've ever felt alone in your grief, this devotion is for you. If you've ever felt like no one was really listening to you, this devotion is for you. If you've ever wished that someone could rise up to defend you against the world's biases, boxes, and barriers, this devotion is for you.

Everyone wants to feel that they have someone to count on, especially during difficult times. We'd like to have an advocate, someone who can cheer us on. My heart certainly craved that advocate relationship during my time of grief. But as I reflect on the entire process, I've become certain of this: My heart is spoken for. Your heart is spoken for! Check it out:

> You are a chosen people, a royal priesthood, a holy nation, God special possession, that you may declare the praises of him who called you out of darkness into his wonderful light. Once you were not a people, but now you are the people of God; once you had not received mercy, but now you have received mercy.
> (1 Peter 2:9,10)

God has chosen us and claimed us as his own. We don't need to fear the isolation of grief any longer. We don't need to fear the consequences of sin any longer. When Jesus stretched out his arms on the cross, his eyes looked at you and he said, "You are mine." Your heart is spoken for! What an amazing example of his unfailing love and mercy!

Because Christ has spoken for you, he is now your great advocate and champion. As Romans 8:34 tells us, "Who then is the one who condemns? No one. Christ Jesus who died—more than that, who was raised to life—is at the right hand of God and is also interceding for us." You have an advocate. You have a perfect listener. So on those days when you feel lonely, overwhelmed, and at a loss for words, know that Christ is rising up to defend you and empower you. Your heart is spoken for!

Prayer: *Dear Lord, thank you for being my advocate and champion. Thank you for claiming me as your own! I rejoice in the peace and comfort I find in you. Amen.*

■ **Reflect:** What issues, emotions, or frustrations would you most like to share with your Advocate today? Lift up these concerns in prayer, knowing that Jesus hears your every word.

■ **Release:** Think of someone in your life who could use an advocate. How might you act on that person's behalf today? Perhaps you could offer a listening ear. Perhaps you could let that person know you're praying for him or her. Be creative, and offer your servant's heart!

WEEK 7

DAY 1 My Heart Rejoices in Your Salvation

Welcome to week 7! Our theme for this week is about rejoicing in God's promise of salvation (Psalm 13:5). As we near the end of our journey, I pray that you're feeling some hope and that positive feelings are building. It's amazing at this stage to look back and recall the somber tone of those early themes based on the opening words of Psalm 13: "How long, LORD? Will you forget me forever? How long will you hide your face from me? How long must I wrestle with my thoughts and day after day have sorrow in my heart? How long will my enemy triumph over me?" (Psalm 13:1,2).

And just think, the same psalmist who wrote these weighty questions just a few short verses earlier penned the uplifting words that stand as our theme for today: "My heart rejoices in your salvation" (13:5)! I'm hoping that as you've read the devotions and reflected on your grief, you've reached a place where you can honestly say to the Lord, "My heart rejoices in your salvation!" Isaiah presents a fantastic, joyful illustration of what it means to rejoice in the Lord's salvation:

> *I delight greatly in the LORD; my soul rejoices*
> *in my God. For he has clothed me with gar-*
> *ments of salvation and arrayed me in a robe of*
> *righteousness, as a bridegroom adorns his head*

> *like a priest, and as a bride adorns herself with*
> *her jewels. (Isaiah 61:10)*

What an awesome image! Close your eyes and picture yourself being clothed by God in your garments of salvation. He's stripped you of your sinfulness. He's washed away every stain, scar, blemish, or imperfection in your heart. He's clothed you as his bride! (No one has impeccable fashion sense like our amazing God!)

When you picture yourself being clothed with salvation this way, how can your heart help but rejoice? When you picture the people you've lost being clothed with salvation this way, how can your heart help but rejoice?

Prayer: *Dear heavenly Father, I praise you for your wisdom, might, and power. I praise you for your glorious plan of salvation. I praise you for washing me clean and clothing me with your salvation. My heart rejoices in you! Amen.*

▓ **Reflect:** Make a list of the differences between the early stages of your grief and what you experience now. Are you surprised at the difference? Take a moment to thank the Lord for the progress he's brought about in your heart. Then take another moment to lay your heart's concerns at the foot of his cross.

■ **Release:** Imagine yourself as a fashion designer charged with creating two outfits. The first design should reflect how you felt when you first experienced loss. How would you capture your emotions in that design? The second outfit should embrace the image of "garments of salvation" and "a robe of righteousness" we read about in Isaiah 61:10. What can you see in your imagination? Better yet, can you draw your designs?

DAY 2 In Christ Alone

While this devotion was easy to write, the message has had a profound impact on my life. Only through Christ can we and the loved ones we lost triumph over death and the grave. Only through Christ do I have the strength to cope with grief and allow him to change my heart. Only through Christ can I reach others with the saving message of his love! Because of this powerful message, today's devotion features the words of the hymn "In Christ Alone" (written by Keith Getty and Stuart Townend).

In Christ alone my hope is found.
He is my light, my strength, my song;
this cornerstone, this solid ground,
firm through the fiercest drought and storm.
What heights of love, what depths of peace,
when fears are stilled, when strivings cease!
My Comforter, my all in all,
here in the love of Christ I stand.

In Christ alone—who took on flesh,
fullness of God in helpless babe!
This gift of love and righteousness,
scorned by the ones he came to save.
Till on that cross, as Jesus died,
the wrath of God was satisfied;
for every sin on Him was laid.
Here in the death of Christ I live.

There in the ground His body lay,
light of the world by darkness slain;
then bursting forth in glorious day
up from the grave he rose again!
And as he stands in victory,
sin's curse has lost its grip on me.

For I am his and he is mine—
bought with the precious blood of Christ.

No guilt in life, no fear in death,
this is the pow'r of Christ in me;
from life's first cry to final breath,
Jesus commands my destiny.
No pow'r of hell, no scheme of man
can ever pluck me from His hand;
till He returns or calls me home,
here in the power of Christ I'll stand.

Amen to that! I pray that this beautiful portrayal of the gospel message has inspired you as much as it has me!

Prayer: *Dear Father in heaven, thank you for the gracious gift of your Son, Jesus Christ. Through him alone, I have forgiveness, peace, and the promise of heaven. Amen.*

Reflect: How does your heart respond to the words of this song today? In what ways has your grieving process been accomplished "In Christ Alone"?

Release: The last stanza closes with the words "Till he returns or calls me home, here in the power of Christ I'll stand." Knowing that you have the power of Christ supporting you, whom can you reach out to today with this awesome message?

DAY 3 The Victory Is Yours!

When was the last time you declared a victory in your life? What have you conquered? Whether it's winning a sporting event or a board game, landing a big contract, or putting away the last load of a mountain of laundry, we all love moments of victory, accomplishment, and the sense of satisfaction for a job well done. What was your most recent victory?

When it comes to grief and loss, it's easy to lose sight of the victories in our lives, especially those that are small or inconsequential. We might be tempted to think, *So what? Nothing seems to overpower my feelings of loss right now.* But if we allow ourselves to lose sight of victory, we might be missing out on the greatest victory of all. " 'Death has been swallowed up in victory.' 'Where, O death, is your victory? Where, O death, is your sting?' The sting of death is sin, and the power of sin is the law. But thanks be to God! He gives us the victory through our Lord Jesus Christ" (1 Corinthians 15:54-57).

Jesus conquered death for us through his innocent suffering—his undeserved punishment for our sins—and his glorious resurrection from the dead on Easter morning. What's awesome about this victory is that it's not something I have to strive for, work for, or earn. God gives me this victory over sin and death. He gives you that victory over sin and death. He gave that victory to our loved ones in heaven. It's just another example of his unfailing love! Christ took the sting out of death; he rendered it completely powerless over those who trust in his name!

While it's important to celebrate our small victories on earth, it's even more important to celebrate the eternal victory you have through Christ! The victory is yours!

Prayer: *Dear Lord, thank you for declaring victory over sin and death in my place! Remind me to celebrate your blessings in my life, especially the blessing of knowing that heaven awaits. Amen.*

■ **Reflect:** What was the last personal event or accomplishment you celebrated? How did you celebrate?

■ **Release:** Plan a celebration of what God has done through your grieving process thus far. You can decide whether to observe this celebration alone or with others, in public or in the comfort of your home, and whether it will be a small celebration or a more dramatic recognition. What's important with this exercise is that you take the time to pause and celebrate God's hand at work in your life.

DAY 4 The Hope of Heaven

Okay, it's time for a gut check. For a while now, we have been working through this grieving process together. The ultimate goal is to gradually change the *self-focus* that characterized the early period of our grief into a *God-focus* that can go the distance. Let's lift our gaze from the ground. Let's abandon our downcast expressions and allow a glimmer of hope to shine in our eyes.

Embrace this transformation, my friends! Lift your eyes to the One who has given you the hope of heaven! To remind you of how certain that hope is, read the following description of the coming of the Lord from 1 Thessalonians 4:13-17:

> *Brothers and sisters, we do not want you to be uninformed about those who sleep in death, so that you do not grieve like the rest of mankind, who have no hope. For we believe that Jesus died and rose again, and so we believe that God will bring with Jesus those who have fallen asleep in him. According to the Lord's word, we tell you that we who are still alive, who are left until the coming of the Lord, will certainly not precede those who have fallen asleep. For the Lord himself will come down from heaven, with a loud command, with the voice of the archangel and with the trumpet call of God, and the dead in Christ will rise first. After that, we who are still alive and are left will be caught up together with them in the clouds to meet the Lord in the air. And so we will be with the Lord forever.*

God has given us his word—our hope is secure. We will be with the Lord forever! We don't need to grieve as someone might who doesn't have this faith foundation. Rather, we grieve with our eyes looking up in hope. We have full confidence that because Jesus died and rose again for us all, the loved one we mourn will rise again as well! That assurance is for you. For you! So look heavenward and wait upon the Lord; he will return! In him, we have been set free from our sins. Because of him, we need not fear the grave. Through him, we have the hope of heaven.

Prayer:

My hope is built on nothing less
than Jesus' blood and righteousness;
I dare to make no other claim
but wholly lean on Jesus' name.
On Christ, the solid rock, I stand;
all other ground is sinking sand.

When darkness veils his lovely face,
I rest on his unchanging grace;
in ev'ry high and stormy gale
my anchor holds within the veil.
On Christ, the solid rock, I stand;
all other ground is sinking sand.

His oath, his covenant and blood,
support me in the raging flood;
when ev'ry earthly prop gives way,
he then is all my hope and stay.
On Christ, the solid rock, I stand;
all other ground is sinking sand.

When He shall come with trumpet sound,
oh, may I then in him be found,
clothed in his righteousness alone,
faultless to stand before his throne.
On Christ, the solid rock I stand;
all other ground is sinking sand. Amen!
("My Hope Is Built on Nothing Less": stanzas 1-4)

■ **Reflect:** Today's devotion offered you a gut-check moment: In what ways have you fulfilled our grieving goal of shifting from the early self-focus to an enduring God-focus? Write an open, honest response to this question.

■ **Release:** If there are still aspects of your grief that you need to surrender to him, write them down and remember them during your prayer time today. As you pray, surrender these concerns with a hope-filled spirit!

DAY 5 Fly to Jesus

Today's devotion is especially personal, but I want to share a moment with you. It's from the heart and about the heart. We can think about the heart from many different perspectives. We refer to the heart as the collective emotions we feel toward someone or something or the part of the anatomy that sustains life with its beat.

Right after my most difficult loss, I remember wondering when the final moment of life had occurred for my baby. When was that final heartbeat? (To an expecting mother, the heartbeat is the measure of life.) And once that final heartbeat sounded, what did that little one experience?

The truth is, when we lose a loved one, many questions come to mind. Some of them won't be answered on this side of heaven.

In my own heart, I imagined that little one being caught up in the warmth of the Father's arms. I imagined the freedom from life's burdens. And I imagined heaven rejoicing that my little one was safely home. The answer to these questions we leave to a God of mercy who loves us because of Jesus!

Perhaps you've had similar reflections about the heart of loss. When was the final heartbeat? What did your own heart experience on behalf of the one you'd lost? Through Christ, we have the confidence that while our final heartbeats may be the end of life on earth, they are the beginning of an eternal life in the perfection of heaven. Now we too can say with the psalmist, "My heart rejoices in your salvation" (Psalm 13:5). Fly to Jesus!

Prayer: *Dear Jesus, thank you for coming to earth as our ransom. Because of you, we know that your loving arms await us in our heavenly home. My heart rejoices in your promises! Amen.*

■ **Reflect:** If you remember your early reflections about your loss, write them down. What did your heart experience? What questions did you ask?

■ **Release:** Find a quiet place and close your eyes for a few minutes. Feel the rhythm of your heartbeat. As you do, ponder the amazing truth that God ordains each and every one of those heartbeats, and he will do so until his purpose for your life on this earth is complete. Pray boldly that he uses you to advance the gospel today!

DAY 6 Family Reunion

Remember how great the first hug feels after you've been away from a loved one for a while? I certainly do! My husband used to travel overseas for work several times a year, usually for seven to ten days at a time. While he was away, my arms longed to wrap around him in a great big hug. I'd imagine that moment at the airport when our eyes would finally meet and I could run and throw my arms around him. Those reunions were tough to wait for; the anticipation was overwhelming. But boy did that reuniting moment make all of the frustrations disappear! Can you remember a moment like that?

As I think back to my husband's travels for work, I can draw a comparison to Christian loss. The loved ones we've lost are waiting at home in the perfection of heaven. Their earthly work for God's kingdom is done. The rest of us are still at work, living and laboring under the Great Commission—in one way or another sharing the good news of the gospel message.

So let's carry on with our mission until the day God declares that our work is done. At that moment, we'll experience a family reunion like none we have ever experienced. While our earthly reunions are very special, they pale in comparison to the family reunion that will be ours through Christ!

God assures us in his Word that we will celebrate a heavenly family reunion with our brothers and sisters in Christ. "Christ has indeed been raised from the dead, the firstfruits of those who have fallen asleep. For since death came through a man, the resurrection of the dead comes also through a man. For as in Adam all die, so in Christ all will be made alive" (1 Corinthians 15:20-22).

When Jesus rose from the dead, he guaranteed that those who believe in him will also rise from the dead to eternal life. In Christ, all will be made alive! Our heavenly reunion is a certainty!

Prayer: *Dear heavenly Father, today my heart rejoices in the salvation you've given me through your Son, because it guarantees me a family reunion beyond my comprehension. Sometimes it's hard to wait for that reunion. Until you call me home, fill me with a sense of your purpose and the courage to share the gospel. Amen.*

Reflect: Think back to a moment when you had a joyful reunion with someone you love. What did you experience physically and emotionally during that reunion?

Release: Knowing that God still has a calling on your life, how can you serve him today? Find at least one way to brighten someone's day, offer help to someone at church, or reach out to a neighbor. Let God use you!

DAY 7 Living Joy

This week we've been reflecting on the theme "my heart rejoices in your salvation." What does the word *rejoice* mean to you? What does it look like when we rejoice? Are you ready to rejoice? These are a few of the questions that we'll work through in our devotion today.

Technically, the word *rejoice* means to feel joy. While it may be difficult to think of your loss and experience joy at the same time, this week's verse challenges you to look beyond your loss to the empty cross. The grieving person won't find joy if his or her eyes stay focused on the loss itself. Rather, the grieving person finds joy when his or her eyes lift toward the cross and take in its full meaning:

> *Once you were alienated from God and were enemies in your minds because of your evil behavior. But now he has reconciled you by Christ's physical body through death to present you holy in his sight, without blemish and free from accusation—if you continue in your faith, established and firm, and do not move from the hope held out in the gospel. (Colossians 1:21-23)*

Yes, the empty cross is the source of your joy, because it is the source of your salvation! But what does it look like to rejoice? Check out some of the behaviors associated with the living joy we have in Christ:

- *The LORD is my strength and my shield; my heart trusts in him, and he helps me. My heart leaps for joy, and with my song I praise him. (Psalm 28:7)*

- *Clap your hands, all you nations; shout to God with cries of joy. (Psalm 47:1)*

- *Worship the LORD with gladness; come before him with joyful songs. (Psalm 100:2)*

- *"Sing for joy, you heavens, for the LORD has done this; shout aloud, you earth beneath. Burst into song, you mountains, you forests and all your trees, for the LORD has redeemed Jacob, he displays his glory in Israel." (Isaiah 44:23)*

Have you responded to God's grace in your life with joy? Are you living joyfully as a servant of the Almighty? If so, keep leaping for joy, clapping your hands, shouting, singing, and worshiping the Lord with gladness! If not, pray that the Lord would grant you a rich measure of the Holy Spirit to fill you with the joy that comes from knowing you are saved through Jesus Christ.

Prayer: *Dear Lord, forgive me for turning my eyes inward and dwelling on the trials and frustrations of this world. Lift my eyes to the cross so that I may experience the joy of your salvation. May my life be a joyful response to your love! Amen.*

▓ **Reflect:** How would you describe your level of joy at this point in your grief? What aspects of your current life fill you with joy?

▓ **Release:** Choose one of the verses about joy in today's devotion and memorize it. Say it often throughout your day to help you keep your eyes focused on the joy that Christ won for you!

WEEK 8

DAY 1 | I Will Sing to the Lord, for He Has Been Good to Me

Welcome to the final week of our devotions. During this final week, we'll reflect on the final verse of Psalm 13: "I will sing the LORD's praise, for he has been good to me."

These last days of processing our grief together won't be your last days of reflecting on and remembering your loss. But it is my hope that the Lord uses thoughts inspired by the theme this week to remind you of his amazing intentions for you and his plan for your life that reaches beyond our limited human vision.

Though it may feel a little weird, I want you to speak the words of our theme verse out loud. Yep, just do it. As I reflect on my own loss, uttering the words of this verse chokes me up every time. To suggest that our losses could ever be viewed as something good might seem like an injustice to you. But with love for our hearts and souls, God allowed our suffering for that very purpose: to be good to us. Can you recognize the good—God's good—in your experiences?

As we say the familiar words of Psalm 23, we speak of God's unending goodness: "Surely your goodness and love will follow me all the days of my life, and I will dwell in the house of the LORD forever" (v. 6). Though God may have felt distant at the time of your loss, his goodness and love were with you. Though your heart might still hurt, his goodness and love are with you. And though you might face more pain and loss in the future, his goodness and love will be with you.

Yes, God's goodness is certainly evident during our earthly trials. But nowhere is it more evident than in the life, suffering, death, and resurrection of Jesus! Sins gone, debt paid, travel documents to heaven confirmed—all through Jesus! God orchestrated his entire plan of salvation for your good—your eternal good!

The final point of our devotion today is that, like the psalmist, we can sing to the Lord in response to his goodness. "I will sing the LORD's praise, for he has been good to me." Join me, and let your life's response to loss sing the Lord's praises.

> *Shout for joy to the LORD, all the earth.*
> *Worship the LORD with gladness;*
> *come before him with joyful songs.*
> *Know that the LORD is God.*
> *It is he who made us, and we are his;*
> *we are his people, the sheep of his pasture.*
> *Enter his gates with thanksgiving and his courts*
>   *with praise;*
> *give thanks to him and praise his name.*
> *For the LORD is good and his love endures forever;*
> *his faithfulness continues through all generations.*
>   *(Psalm 100)*

Sing to the Lord, for he has been good to you. Through it all, the Lord has, is, and will be good to you!

Prayer: *Dear Lord, I praise you for your goodness! Each and every day help me recognize that your goodness and love truly do follow me all the days of my life. Let my life sing of your goodness. Amen.*

■ **Reflect:** What are the good things God has brought about in your life through this loss? What still hurts the most? Share your answers to both of these questions with your loving Lord in prayer.

■ **Release:** Think of a favorite joyful hymn or song of praise. Play, sing, or listen to that song today as a reminder that God's goodness to you is worthy of praise!

DAY 2 Pouring Out

Have you poured out anything yet today? A cup of juice or milk for a child? Your morning cup of coffee? This may seem obvious, but in order for you to have poured that juice, milk, or coffee, someone must have filled the container.

When you first saw the title of today's devotion, perhaps you thought about all the pouring out you've done as part of the grieving process. We pour out tears. We pour out emotions. We pour out frustrations.

While this outpouring is beneficial and healing for those who grieve, God has more in mind for us than pouring out *our* perspective. He invites us to think about how he has filled us—with hope. To help us understand this, we look at 2 Timothy, where Paul discusses the manner in which he is poured out:

> *I am already being poured out like a drink*
> *offering, and the time for my departure is near.*
> *I have fought the good fight, I have finished the*
> *race, I have kept the faith. Now there is in store*
> *for me the crown of righteousness, which the*
> *Lord, the righteous Judge, will award to me on*
> *that day—and not only to me, but also to all*
> *who have longed for his appearing.*
> *(2 Timothy 4:6-8)*

Here Paul is talking about some Old Testament sacrifices. Drink offerings of wine were poured out in connection with some specific sacrifices. Paul knew that the end of his life was very near. He was going to die as a martyr. The steps that would lead to his martyrdom had already been set in motion. His life was being "poured out" like one of those drink offerings. But look at the words that follow; God had *filled* him with hope—the hope of the resurrection through Jesus Christ. Because God had filled him with hope, Paul would continue to confess the message of Jesus until he received his crown of righteousness.

It is easy for us who grieve to focus on what we need to pour out as we heal. But in his great wisdom, God uses our times of grief to draw us closer to himself and to fill us with the message of Christ and with the hope that message gives us. This message gives us a new perspective and then enables us to use our lips and our lives to his glory. So in addition to the juice, milk, or coffee, pour out your love for Jesus! He has indeed been good to you (Psalm 13:6).

Prayer: *Lord, forgive me for the times when I am self-consumed with pouring out my grief. Fill me with your love, your hope, your grace, and the ability to pour out my praise for Jesus by sharing the gospel with the people around me. Amen.*

▨ Reflect: Consider the fullness of your heart and mind at the present. Are you still allowing your grief to overwhelm you? Are you welcoming God's comfort, direction, and desire to fill you with his message of salvation? Something in between?

▨ Release: Make a pot of coffee or tea today, and as you drink, consider it a metaphor for God's desire to fill you with his love, to warm you with his healing, and to comfort you with the hope of heaven.

DAY 3 Let Your Light Shine

For stage productions, a lot of time is spent getting the lighting just right. Proper lighting helps the audience focus on what should be the center of attention. Lighting can help set the mood.

Today it's your time to shine! The stage is set, and God has beautifully outfitted you for your performance. You are equipped to shine by the Savior who took you out of the darkness of sin and brought you into the light of his salvation! One way he has equipped you to shine is by what you have been through during your grief. Your light has been turned on, so let it shine!

Of course, there are a few key differences between a theatrical performance and God's call on your life to let your light shine. First, your life is to be a consistent, enduring witness, not a limited-time-only performance or a coming attraction. Second, you don't need any fancy stage lights—you are the light! Here's the evidence:

- *"You are the light of the world. A town built on a hill cannot be hidden. Neither do people light a lamp and put it under a bowl. Instead they put it on its stand, and it gives light to everyone in the house. In the same way, let your light shine before others, that they may see your good deeds and glorify your Father in heaven." (Matthew 5:14-16)*

- *"Those who are wise will shine like the brightness of the heavens, and those who lead many to righteousness, like the stars for ever and ever." (Daniel 12:3)*

- *Do everything without grumbling or arguing, so that you may become blameless and pure, 'children of God without fault in a warped and crooked generation.' Then you will shine among them like stars in the sky as you hold firmly to the word of life. (Philippians 2:14-16a)*

God has called each of us to live our lives as shining examples of faith so that we might draw others to him. Don't hide your light in the darkness you felt surrounding your grief. Let it shine for all to see, especially for those who need hope and inspiration to make it through their own struggles. Shine so that all the world can see the loving face and the nail-pierced hands of Jesus.

Prayer: *Dear Lord, forgive me for the times when I've been self-ish, reserved, or complacent about letting my light shine for others. Empower me by your Spirit to proclaim what you have done in my life and for the salvation of all. Amen.*

Reflect: Think of a person in your life who has been an example for you of what it means to live out faith as a witness to others. With a spirit of gratitude, identify the ways in which this person's example has inspired or impacted you.

Release: Find a way to thank the person you identified in your reflection exercise today; be specific when describing the impact he or she has had on your life.

DAY 4 Remembering

As our time together draws to a close, I encourage you to remember. Remember where you were physically, mentally, emotionally, and spiritually during the early stages of your grief. Remember the turning points you've had along the way: those moments when God opened your eyes to a piece of his plan, empowered you to tell your story, or simply drew you closer to himself. And remember the person you are right now as you move into the future.

Beyond remembering your journey, remember your loved one. Remember the feelings of gladness you had during time spent together. Remember the joy you shared with family and friends. Remember the smiles, the personality, and the bond. Remember God's creation.

Remember the purpose of your loss: to draw you closer, to refine you, and to equip you for service to your Savior. He has been good to you! (Psalm 13:6).

When you remember your grief, your loved one, and the purpose of your loss, remember the loving God who carried you along the way. Remember the gracious God who, through his Son, Jesus, promised to forget every one of your sins! Find comfort in the psalmist's words: "He has remembered his love and his faithfulness to Israel; all the ends of the earth have seen the salvation of our God" (Psalm 98:3). When he looks at you, he looks at you with love. He looks at you with faithfulness. He looks at you as his holy, redeemed child. That's how he remembers you!

So remember him! Remember the One who knows where you've been and who holds your future in his hands.

Prayer: *Dear heavenly Father, when I am tempted to forget all that you've accomplished in my life, help me to remember your love and faithfulness. Continue to draw me closer to you every day! Amen.*

■ **Reflect:** Describe what it feels like to remember your feelings and your struggles at the beginning of the grieving process. How have you changed? Describe what it's like to remember your loved one at this point in your grief. How have you changed the way you frame your loss?

■ **Release:** Spend some time looking through photos, scrapbook pages, or other items you've kept to help you remember your loved one. As you do, know that God holds your heart. Share the experience and the memories with him in prayer!

DAY 5 | A Spirit of Celebration

Are you ready to celebrate? We're almost there!

When I think of the word *celebrate,* I think of a song by Kenny Loggins that's frequently played around Christmastime. It's called "Celebrate Me Home." It's about a person far-removed from his loved ones who wishes that somehow his family's spirit of celebration could bring him home. (It's always difficult to be away from those we love, but the holidays seem to bring out those feelings even more!)

Yesterday we talked about remembering those we've lost. Today we'll take it one step further and *celebrate those loved ones home* in our memories. Let's celebrate who our loved ones were and what they meant to us. Let's celebrate them as God's workmanship. Let's celebrate them as lives that were meant to influence us on our spiritual journeys. Think of words written in the book of Ephesians: "We are God's handiwork, created in Christ Jesus to do good works, which God prepared in advance for us to do" (2:10). The end of life is also an opportunity for God to accomplish his purposes through us!

While we celebrate our loved ones home through our memories, let's also celebrate that our loved ones are in their eternal home in heaven: "Praise be to the God and Father of our Lord Jesus Christ! In his great mercy he has given us new birth into a living hope through the resurrection of Jesus Christ from the dead, and into an inheritance that can never perish, spoil or fade. This inheritance is kept in heaven for you, who through faith are shielded by God's power until the coming of the salvation that is ready to be revealed in the last time" (1 Peter 1:3-5). Our loved ones are already experiencing this inheritance, and we will join them according to God's perfect timing. This hope is certain!

Because of Christ's death and resurrection, we can celebrate life. We can celebrate the lives of those who have been with us. We can celebrate the memories that keep that life with us. But, most important, we can celebrate the eternal life that our loved ones are living; we can celebrate that they are home!

Prayer: *Dear heavenly Father, I thank you for making it possible, through your Son, Jesus, to celebrate the fact that the loved ones I've lost are at home with you in heaven. Thank you also for the ability to celebrate life through the blessing of memories. Amen.*

■ **Reflect:** It's striking to me that God can use the end of someone's earthly life to accomplish his purposes, sometimes to a greater degree than when the person was still alive. How has God accomplished his purposes in your life through this loss?

■ **Release:** Read the verses from 1 Peter 1:3-5 again, and write down what these verses mean to you as you think of both your loved one and yourself.

DAY 6 The Finish Line

For today's devotion, we'll be considering the words in Acts 20:24: "I consider my life worth nothing to me; my only aim is to finish the race and complete the task the Lord Jesus has given me—the task of testifying to the good news of God's grace."

If you've ever trained for a race, I'm sure that you have daydreamed about what it would be like to cross the finish line. Perhaps you imagined hearing crowds of people cheering for you as you take the final steps. Perhaps you imagined how your body would feel, used up but with a definite sense of accomplishment. Perhaps you imagined that special someone reaching out to you to say, "Well done!" Or perhaps your daydream was simply a collection of all the emotions you might feel upon finishing the race.

In our verse for today, the writer says that the only reason for his existence is to finish the race—his God-given task of testifying to the gospel. Could you imagine an earthly race that would be your only reason for living? Thank goodness that isn't the case! There are many things that could keep us from finishing an earthly race. But Jesus' words—"It is finished"—remind us that he crossed the finish line that really matters in our place! And because of him, our loved ones have crossed that same finish line into the peace and perfection of heaven!

We know that we're here for more than our earthly races. We know that God still has a calling on our lives. God gives us each the task of testifying to the gospel, and he will use our lives— whatever it takes—to turn us into his instruments to pass on the news of his grace. In that sense, consider God the best personal trainer you could ask for!

Whatever vision you've had of what it's like to cross a finish line on race day, nothing compares to what it will be like for us to cross the finish line into eternity. Your loved one and all those who have died with faith will be there. The body you've beaten and worn will be pain-free and perfect. That special someone—our heavenly Father—will be reaching out to you and declaring "Well done, good and faithful servant!"

Prayer: *Lord Jesus, thank you for finishing the earthly race as my substitute! Guide me as I finish the race and complete the task that you've given me of testifying to your grace! Amen.*

■ **Reflect:** What might God be calling you to accomplish as you make your way through your race course on this earth? Make a list of some service interests or opportunities that would allow you to reach others with the gospel.

■ **Release:** Choose one of the ideas you created in your reflection exercise and take the first step toward making it a reality.

DAY 7 The Conclusion of the Matter

I distinctly remember a moment during my most difficult loss when my son, a preschooler at the time, looked into my eyes and asked, "Mommy, what's the matter?" That little boy could see the pain of my heart displayed all over my face. What he saw on the outside was a nonverbal translation of what my heart felt on the inside—the emotions expressed in the first verses of Psalm 13:

> *How long, LORD? Will you forget me forever?*
> *How long will you hide your face from me?*
> *How long must I wrestle with my thoughts*
> *and day after day have sorrow in my heart?*
> *How long will my enemy triumph over me?*
> *(vv. 1,2)*

What was the matter with me? Loss was the matter. Uncertainty was the matter. Sin was the matter. In God's great mercy, he knew just what to do about this matter, and the conclusion of the matter is this: God's love extends so far toward us that he suffered the loss of his own Son to erase what was "the matter" with us— with all of us. Because of his grace, we are now free to serve him during the next phase of our lives.

Speaking of the next phase, can you believe that you are turning to the last page of this devotional? Turning to the "last page" of a phase of life can be intimidating and overwhelming. If you're like me, the last page often causes me to ask, "What's next?" My quest for certainty in response to this question is much like my early contemplation of Psalm 13:3,4:

> *Look on me and answer, LORD my God.*
> *Give light to my eyes, or I will sleep in death,*
> *and my enemy will say, "I have overcome him,"*
> *and my foes will rejoice when I fall.*

In the face of the question about what's next, we have a choice before God. We can crumble under the pressure such a big question brings with it, or with humility and gratitude, acknowledging that we are servants of the One who has a calling on our lives, we can embrace the possibilities of what's next. If I take a moment to look back on my life one phase at a time, I see my loving God guiding and directing me through each one. He didn't leave me stranded. He didn't leave me alone. Can you see that he's done the same for you? Let's rejoice together that we serve such a faithful God, and let's reflect on what he's done for us during this time of loss:

> But I trust in your unfailing love;
> my heart rejoices in your salvation.
> I will sing the LORD's praise,
> for he has been good to me. (Psalm 13:5-6)

God has been good to me. God has been good to you. It has been such a tremendous blessing for me to share these devotions with you, and I pray that God has used them to draw you close and remind you that he's always at your side. Now it's time to let your life sing his praises! Share the goodness that God has accomplished in your life.

Prayer: *Dear heavenly Father, I am so grateful for this opportunity to grow closer to you. I praise you for your wisdom in guiding all things for my eternal good. I praise you for taking my "matters" into your hands and freeing me to serve you here on earth and forever in heaven. Fill me with your Holy Spirit as I embrace your purposes for my life. Be my light and guide me to where you need me most. Let my life sing for you! Amen.*